Irish Theatre International

in association with
the Irish Society for
Theatre Research

Irish Theatre International **is published by Carysfort Press for the Irish Society for Theatre Research**

Published by Carysfort Press Ltd, in association with Peter Lang

58 Woodfield, Scholarstown Road,
Dublin 16, Ireland

ISBN 978-1-78874-815-5

Irish Theatre International

CONTENTS

Editorial

MIRIAM HAUGHTON, MARIA KURDI

Perform, Or Else!

> *'Freedom [...] is a very good horse to ride, but to ride somewhere'.*
> Matthew Arnold, *Culture and Anarchy (1869)*

This latest issue of *Irish Theatre International* bridges the discourses of theatre practice and research with that of performance studies, and also with the ways in which social, economic, political and cultural activities perform their needs and demands. Recent decades honed these links through the 'turn to performance' markedly explored in the US since the 1960s, as ideas of play, ritual, and performativity flowered and cross-pollinated the humanities and indeed, scientific disciplines, crossing shores and attracting a global reach. This bridge specifically locates these interdisciplinary enquiries in the context of neoliberal economic cultures pervading the western world and further afield, produced and managed under the costume of 'freedom'. Neoliberal engineers and advocates argue for the economic and social benefits such policies offer, foregrounding their argument around the notion of 'freedom'. Freedom is a human right, a moral imperative, and a symbol of progress in civilization. As David Harvey summarizes, 'The founding figures of neoliberal thought took political ideals of human dignity and individual freedom as fundamental, as "the central values of civilization" [...] These values, they held, were threatened not only by fascism, dictatorships, and communism, but by all forms of state intervention that substituted collective judgements for those of individuals free to choose' (*A Brief History of Neoliberalism* [Oxford: Oxford University Press, 2005], p. 5).

The language of neoliberalism is tempting, and its narrative appealing; increased private wealth, globalized connections, and virtual worlds alongside physical encounters where commerce can expand – in theory. As performance scholars are all too well aware, in practice, performances can live and grow separate to the control of their auteurs, gather pace and produce unanticipated responses. Each performance is unique, as is each audience. Fundamentally, this cultural moment is enveloped in a framework of pressure and threat, 'perform – or else'. This threat dominates the arts and academia as well as commercial fields, territorializing all aspects of public life as 'industry', thus treating citizens as consumers, and equating value with wealth and profit. Ireland is no exception. Nations and communities wield less power over the performance of everyday life than multinationals; what impact can individual presence and action still achieve? This is where the realm of theatre research and sites of performance provide pathways of enquiry and response.

Throughout the scope of this issue, these interwoven interdisciplinary dialogues present a querying of value systems in modern and contemporary Irish theatre and performance, and their relationship to Irish culture, society and global politics. Paradigm-shifts in theatre-making and the arts in Ireland since the early twentieth century are potently responding to this culture of pressure, consumption and manipulation of the scope of the term 'performance' through producing work marked by instances of interrogation, exposure, and resistance. Politically and economically, the 'Celtic Tiger' performance of Ireland crashed in 2009, resulting in global recognition as a member of the EU 'PIIGS' [Portugal, Ireland, Italy, Greece, Spain] category. In a matter of months, the international branding of the nation jumped from Celtic Tiger to Kitten. Socially, individuals and communities struggled to cope with performing daily tasks and rituals. Artistically, the same period is incredibly rich. While Arts Council funding and other supports have been heavily penalized, many artists and companies survive due to the increasing audience interest in their challenging work. As the momentum of institutional collapse in Ireland roars ahead, the ritual, celebration, and critique facilitated by the arts offers, in varying degrees, access to encounters of integrity, dignity, exposure, truth and community to a shaken Irish society. 'Boom' indeed; the sound of cannon fire on a battlefield. The battlefield is a play for power, where dominant ideas and organizations vie for control and do so under the guise of 'this is good for you'. In this 'democracy', the stronger are not protecting the weaker. Performing 'freedom' through Ireland's neoliberal policies has failed. What horse do we ride now, and in which direction?

At the annual Irish Society for Theatre Research conference in 2012 hosted by NUI Galway, themed 'Perform, or Else!', the call for papers declared that performance 'is how a neo-liberal service economy measures failure or success'. Noting the political under-theorization of this term in Irish theatre and performance, the conference asked how might 'the terms and conditions of the theatrical encounter as imagined by dramatists, directors and performers clarify and/or expand an understanding of social and political value?' Value is the key word in this question, and reflects the overarching enquiry in each of the forthcoming essays, the first versions or parts of which were presented at the conference. Interrogating a culture of performance on and off stage in a neoliberal climate manifests as an investigation and analysis of value systems between people and place. Activities and relationships often appearing insignificant and everyday through the veneer of habit, dominant attitudes and everyday social practice, become scrutinized in performance, resisting and disrupting normalized and naturalized patterns of viewing and thinking.

It is hardly possible to scrutinize the present without pointing back to the past, which often results in a sense of continuity. The first article in the present issue, 'The Cries of Pagan Desperation' by Chris Collins, is concerned with the way in which J. M. Synge uses the performance of the pre-Christian Gaelic ritual of keening in *Riders to the Sea*. In 1904, when the play was first performed, revitalizing this tradition for the stage challenged the cultural expectations dictated by the powerful Catholic Church and its influence on nationalist ideas about theatre. 'Pre-Christian residual culture could be instrumental in the articulation of state-orientated nationalism. However, if the pre-Christian fantasy of the Celtic Geist materialized as pre-Christian reality then it was promptly removed from cultural hegemony, because its apparent pre-political logic was problematical for the habitations of Catholic, bourgeois modernity' Collins writes. Performance in Synge's work, thus, assumes a disruptive, critical role and intervenes in the univocal, restrictive power and value systems of the bourgeois nationalists, potential ancestors of today's neoliberals in Ireland.

Indeed, Siobhan O'Gorman's essay 'Scenographic Interactions' marks the roots of Ireland's turn to western first world economics in the 1950s, seeking the leadership and expertise of economics from the world stage. Employing the Pike Theatre's scenographic histories and wider Irish visual culture as case studies, O'Gorman interrogates how what we see is prepared images, moulded, informed and reflecting a much larger canvas. Placing these design and performance histories among the cultural critique of 1950s tells a wider narrative; one that encompasses policy making at government level, during an era when Ireland moved from economic isolation to a global marketplace. Thus, O'Gorman maps a turning point in Ireland's economic policies, which are fundamental to the present-day pressures to perform. Considering the role of multiple state organizations, she argues, 'These organizations harnessed visual and theatrical culture to enhance Ireland's performance on the international stage, and to promote what can now be seen as a revisionist questioning of established constructions of Irishness'.

Jumping to the present post-millennium and post-Celtic Tiger era, Lisa Fitzgerald's essay presents how fifty-odd years on, Ireland's international economics imprints everyday artistic practice and cultural consumption. She acutely reviews the policies of the Arts Council in her essay 'Uneasy Bedfellows', bringing the daily challenges and complexities of Ireland's venues and theatre-makers to the fore. Through analysis of 'creative clustering' in recent years and the 'production hub' model encouraged through recent Arts Council policies, Fitzgerald asserts that while economic funding to the arts must be sustainable, at the same time, fears are widespread that ultimately, 'the sporadic and somewhat nomadic work of the production hubs model and the clustering of theatre practitioners in varying projects will destabilize a successful framework for theatre making'.

Eamonn Jordan has appropriately chosen 'Respond or Else' as the title of his analysis of Conor McPherson's *The Weir* at the Donmar Warehouse, London, 2013. Performances elicit responses of many kinds, which then have an immense role in alerting theatre people as well as authors to audience needs and the possibility to influence those needs. While providing a highly perceptive analysis of the revival of *The Weir* directed by Josie Rourke, with attention to all kinds of theatrical detail, Jordan raises important and also intrusive questions about what critics and audience members bring with them to the theatre, which will then manipulate their responses. Among so much else, '[t]here can be problems with being over-familiar with a work, less emotionally engaged, less easily instinctive and also perhaps overly anticipative in one's responses' Jordan warns. The endless range of responses and interpretations are both culturally and economically embedded, therefore, to continue this train of thought, they are not at all free, irrespective of how subjective they may seem, from the influence of the larger political milieu, its values and constraints.

'Gay Masculinities in Performance: Towards a Queer Dramaturgy' by Cormac O'Brien has most of the above mentioned strands in its hold. O'Brien analyses some contemporary Irish plays and performances which address issues of gay identity and subjectivity utilizing conventional and experimental strategies respectively. The former evoke neoliberal pressures towards assimilation, whereas the latter place emphasis on performativity as a force to contest commodified versions and fixities of Irish masculinity. The author argues that 'there has been a recent shift in performances of gay masculinities in Irish theatrical culture', which can be identified 'as a move from gay dramas into queer theatre'. This move is evaluated as a healthy one, liberating theatre and performance from the evolving 'homonormativity' in neoliberal cultures. To a degree, 'homonormativity' works similarly to bourgeois nationalism which, in Synge's time and later, restricted the conception of Irish identity to purify and homogenize it in the interest of what its representatives thought was progress and (national) freedom.

This collection of papers would not be complete without the striking contribution of Neil Watkins, an Irish theatre maker's reflections regarding how he experienced a call to 'Perform, Or Else!' amidst the problems with selfhood he confronts. His piece delves into the sensitive issue of artistic freedom, implying the imperative to constantly revise assumptions about what performance might/should mean to performers, spectators, critics and those in charge of distributing funds for cultural production to be consumed by different layers of the society. 'Art, art, art, is suffering because of self-consciousness, fear and ego. And the standard from the Irish Institutions is sending out the wrong message to the masses. Work is too often soulless', Watkins rightly warns us.

When scholars, theatre makers and communities turn to the archives of our theatre and performance history in 100 years, what will the records tell them? Early in the twentieth century, during the creative lifetime of Synge, the island of Ireland was under the rule of the British Empire, and factions throughout the nation were readying themselves for resistance against colonialism; ruling forces which prevented society existing in the 'freedom' preferable to them. These experiences and histories were captured, complicated and contested through the plays and artworks of politicized playwrights, poets and individuals. They tell of action and consequence, short-term and long-term. In 2014, notions of freedom remain pivotal to how we govern and live on this island, among neighbours and on distant shores. Will the theatre of today, produced in a climate of neoliberal policy and centralized European hegemony, further complicated by remnants of patriarchal Irish laws and customs, be a strange story to the future civilization, or a familiar one? Publications like the present one with its inquisitive material will hopefully survive and tell future readers, some perhaps our representatives, about the interface between theatre studies discourse, performance, society and economy in our time.

As guest editors we express gratitude to the president of ISTR, Dr Melissa Sihra, for asking us to guest edit this significant issue. Thanks are due to the authors as well, including theatre maker Neil Watkins, who have answered the call and are bringing fresh insights to the broad theme of 'Perform, Or Else!' in their papers. Further, we thank members of the ITI advisory board who were ready to become involved in the peer-reviewing process of the papers and offered the authors (and editors) valuable advice and suggestions about revisions. Finally, we are grateful to Carysfort Press and the Arts Council Ireland/An Chomhairle Ealaíon for generously assisting and supporting the publication of this journal issue, which would not have materialized without their kind consideration and efforts. We hope it offers as much value to its readers as it has to its editors and authors, making Irish theatre research and practice all the richer, in uncertain yet provocative times.

'The Cries of Pagan Desperation': Synge, *Riders to the Sea* and the Discontents of Historical Time

CHRISTOPHER COLLINS

This essay considers Synge's staging of the caoine (keen) in *Riders to the Sea* (1904). It argues that the caoine in *Riders to the Sea* is not simply an aesthetic and unethical fetishization of pre-Christian cultural residue predicated on class insecurity, but a performance philosophy of modernity. Synge's knowledge of caoineadh (keening) as a cultural performance, and as an object of academic study, is contextualized using various unpublished manuscripts in order to demonstrate how the caoine in the Ireland of Synge's time was considered to be the discontents of historical time. Unorthodox histories summon unorthodox temporalities and, in *Riders to the Sea*, it is argued that Synge called forth an alternative temporality of modernity that punctured and punctuated dominant specularity whether that was Anglo-Irish or Catholic in its gaze.

> I feel historical plays are an absolute necessaity [sic] here
> if the drama is to take a grip of the people and if I don't
> succeed I will prepare the way for someone else
> -Lady Gregory.[1]
>
> The moment the sense of historical truth awakes
> in Europe historical fiction becomes impossible
> -J.M. Synge.[2]

Victorians were fascinated with the measurement of time. Everything needed to be clocked: from the time it took the Galway train to travel to Dublin, to those residual cultures of the Empire that had supposedly failed to evolve. J.M. Synge

---

[1] Lady Augusta Gregory to Wilfrid Scawen Blunt, 16 January 1905. The Henry W. and Albert A. Berg Collection of English and American Literature, The New York Public Library Astor, Lenox and Tilden Foundations: 65b2290, ff.29-30. Hereafter quoted as NYPL MS: and folio number. All quotes come with permission from The New York Public Library.

[2] J.M. Synge, *The J.M. Synge Manuscripts from the Library of Trinity College Dublin*: 4396 f.61r. Hereafter quoted as TCD MS: and folio number. All quotes come with permission from The Board of Trinity College Dublin.

understood that analogue time was not an objective unit of measurement because it is relative to the experience of time in a particular space: spacetime. Spacetime maintains that time cannot be objectively reduced to the slow ticking hands of the clock because, as the saying goes, 'time flies when you are having fun', which is to say the experience of time on, for example, the Galway train is generally relative to that given space. The continuum between space and time relativized Isaac Newton's long-held conception of time as absolute and independent from space and place. Synge was not a theoretical physicist, but his understanding of time was closely aligned to the principles of general relativity: 'the absolute of all sequences is time' Synge agreed, 'but the conception of matter as presented or represented in the developed consciousness involves the conception of space time'.[3] For Synge, the measurement of time was very much dependent on the place of the measurer within a given space. The aim of this essay is to consider Synge's understanding of the relativity of time in relation to the performativity of forgotten history.

Alternative spaces summon alternative temporalities. In years to come, Martin Heidegger would argue that the objectivity of time (*vorhanden*) is only possible because of our being in time (*Dasein*): 'time is not something that I encounter out there in the world, but is what I myself am [...] time characterizes the whole of Dasein'.[4] Temporalities are alternative because they are unique and subjective access points to the matrixes of memory that frame the hegemony of historical narrative. Synge's plays articulate alternative temporalities because they are predicated upon pre-Christian cultural memories that are incommensurate with the objective time of Catholic modernity that continually clocked progress. Cardinal Paul Cullen's Devotional Revolution (1850-75) modernized the Catholic Church in Ireland by implementing Roman Orthodoxy, therefore halting the recourse to popular pre-Christian cultural practises. But such insistence on the orthodoxy of Catholic temporality was never going to sit comfortably with Synge, and he looked towards those places and spaces of residual pre-Christian culture where time seemingly stood still. Synge's continual return to the pluralization of objective time was very much dependent on articulating the relative logic of those measurements of time that he encountered in a particular space: the Aran Islands. For example, on Aran Synge noticed that 'few of the people, however, are sufficiently used to modern time to understand in more than a vague way the convention of hours, and when I tell them what o'clock it is by my watch they are not satisfied' and furthermore, 'the general knowledge of time on the island depends, curiously enough, on the direction of the wind'.[5] In *Riders to the Sea*, the dramatist drew characters whose measurement of time was specific to their place within the space of *Inis Meáin*. Throughout the play the

[3] TCD MS: 4379 ff.93r-93v.

[4] Martin Heidegger, *Supplements: From the Earliest Essays to Being and Time and Beyond*, ed. John van Buren (New York: State University of New York Press, 2002), p. 169.

[5] J.M. Synge, *Collected Works*, vol. 2, *Prose*, ed. Alan Price (London: Oxford University Press, 1966), p. 66.

idiosyncratic measurement of space-time contemporaneous with Synge's *Inis Meáin* is returned to again and again in order to explain the location of Michael's body, Bartley's absence at the Galway fair and the acuteness of Maurya's loss: from hours, to days, to weeks, to the perpetuity of death, where those that have passed are, in Maurya's famous phrase, 'altogether this time'.[6]

Alternative temporalities summon alternative histories. Synge's dramaturgy in *Riders to the Sea* pluralizes the objectivity of historical time both on and offstage: the past discloses the present, so that the present can remember the future. Jean-Paul Sartre postulated that 'it is the future which decides whether the past is living or dead',[7] and there is one particular performance with a pre-Christian genealogy that Synge mobilized in *Riders to the Sea* in order to remember the future of Irish culture: *caoineadh* (keening). In the performance of *caoineadh,* Synge identified a discrepancy between religious and political ideology. This discrepancy lies in the understanding that Catholic, bourgeois Ireland regulated the performance of pre-Christian sensibilities by equating them with a pre-modern and pre-political consciousness; 'we can conceive', said the staunch Catholic D.P. Moran, 'and we have full tolerance for a Pagan or a non-Catholic Irishman', but by the same token that same person must 'have respect for the potent facts that are bound up with Irish Nationality'.[8] For Synge, vestigial beliefs such as the *caoine* (keen) were anything but pre-modern and pre-political, and his staging of a supposedly out-dated cultural performance was the attempt by an embattled dramatist to remember a ritual that was fast disappearing from cultural memory. Consequently, this essay considers the performance of *caoineadh* in *Riders to the Sea* in relation to Synge's pluralization of absolute time. The performance of the *caoine* in *Riders to the Sea* summons an unorthodox temporality because, as this essay will explain, the performance of the ritual collapses absolute time into a tripartite structure of past/present/future. However, the performance of the *caoine* also summoned the discontents of historical time; *caoineadh* was an aporia within the temporality of Catholic modernity because it was considered heathen. Such temporal interrogations of Catholic modernity proposes an alternative reading of Paul Murphy's expert analysis of Synge's all too evident fetishization of the Irish peasant *qua* fantasy object.[9]

---

[6] J.M. Synge, *Collected Works*, vol. 3, *Plays*, ed. Ann Saddlemyer (London: Oxford University Press, 1968), p. 26.

[7] Jean-Paul Sartre, *Being and Nothingness: An Essay on Phenomenological Ontology*, trans. Hazel E. Barnes (London: Routledge, 2003), p. 520.

[8] D.P. Moran, 'Protestants and the Irish Nation', *Leader*, 27 July 1901.

[9] See Paul Murphy, *Hegemony and Fantasy in Irish Drama, 1899-1949* (Basingstoke: Palgrave MacMillan, 2008), pp. 19-41. Throughout this essay I carefully use the words 'peasant' and 'peasantry', as an index for a rural class that existed outside of the bourgeois habitations of *fin-de-siècle* and early twentieth century Irish modernity.

The Cries of Pagan Desperation

Caoineadh appears in three of Synge's seven plays: *Riders to the Sea*, *The Playboy of the Western* World (1907) and *Deirdre of the Sorrows* (1910). It is also written into the dramaturgy of two of his playlets, *A Vernal Play* (written in 1902-3) and *Luasnad, Capa and Laine* (also written in 1902-3), the latter being inspired by Geoffrey Keating's *caoine* for Mother Ireland. *Caoineadh* holds its provenance within the *nosad* (funeral rites) of the *Teamhur Feis* (Rites of Tara).[10] The *nosad* of the *Teamhur Feis* were conducted by the Arch Druid of Ireland at the burial of the deceased High King of Ireland. St. Patrick usurped the *Teamhur Feis* in 433 A.D., which precipitated pre-Christian culture into a decline from a culture of dominance to a culture of residue. However, *caoineadh* persisted in its counter-normative logic through the ancient saga texts, such as 'Deirdre's Lament for the Sons of Uisneach' or 'Emer's lament for Cú Chulainn', through to the Fenian ballads and, further still, into Dion Boucicault's *The Shaughraun* (1874), and later still into Synge's plays.

In 1670 a Catholic Synod instructed the clergy to erase *caoineadh* from the religious *habitus* because it was anathema to a modernizing, institutional Church that wanted to distance itself from the superstitious hearsay of vernacular Gaelic religion. But despite the Church's role as an ideological state apparatus, *caoineadh* still dominated the religious *habitus*, which precipitated the Diocese of Leighlin, Co. Kildare, to issue their 1748 tract on *caoineadh*:

It is therefore (ordained) all Parish Priests and religious laymen of this Diocese are herby strictly charged and commanded, in virtue of holy obedience, to use all possible means to banish from Christian burials such anti-Christian practices, by imposing arbitrary punishment of prayers, fasting, alms and suchlike wholesome injunctions on as many men and women as will loudly cry and howl at burials. But to such men and women as will or do make it their trade to cry or rhyme at burials, we decree and declare that for the first crime of this kind they shall not be absolved by any but by the Ordinary or his representatives, and in case of a ralapse [sic], the aforesaid criers or rhymers are to be excluded from Mass and the Sacraments, and in case of perseverance in this detestable practice, they are to be excommunicated and denounced.[11]

But these directives had little effect because the Church was trying to erase a ritual performance that had been ingrained on the Irish religious *habitus*. However, the Great Famine was to have a cataclysmic effect on the religious *habitus*, for not only was an entire generation of *ban caointhes* (female keeners) lost, but furthermore, the Church seized its opportunity to juxtapose the Famine against divine retribution. That such an ideology was readily accepted is evident from the accounts collected by the Irish Folklore Commission, in which informants such as John McCarthy of Enniskean,

---

[10] Eugene O'Curry, *On the Manners and Customs of the Ancient Irish*, vol. 1 (Dublin: John F. Fowler, 1874), p. cccxxiv.

[11] M. Comerford, *Collections Relating to The Dioceses of Kildare and Leighlin* (Dublin and London: James Duffy and Sons, 1883), pp. 81-82.

County Cork, recalled that 'the famine [sic] was the will of God.'[12] With the cultural haemorrhage that followed in the wake of the Famine, Irish culture ceased to pervasively operate in the Gaelic way and *caoineadh*, an elementary principle of Gaelic culture, reached a hiatus and then disappeared into the annals of history; George Petrie, the great antiquarian admired by Synge, travelled Ireland during the Famine and despairingly recalled how '"The land of song" was no longer tuneful; or, if a human sound met the traveller's ear, it was only that of the feeble and despairing wail for the dead.'[13]

In 1850 the Catholic Church met in Thurles for their Synodal meeting, and under the leadership of Cardinal Paul Cullen, the Church proceeded to enact its Devotional Revolution. However, cultural formations develop unevenly and according to Seán Ó Súilleabháin the *caoine* persisted in its recalcitrant logic in those pockets that would not, or could not, submit to Catholic modernity's totalizing history of progress:

> My father told me that he attended a funeral in the parish of Tuosist, in South Kerry, at the turn of the [twentieth] century. As the coffin was being taken in a cart to the local graveyard at Kilmackillogue, three women keeners sat on top of it, howling and wailing at intervals. The parish priest, on horseback, met the funeral near Derreen, a few miles from the graveyard, and rode at its head along the road. As soon as he heard the three women howl loudly, he turned his horse around and trotted back until he reached them, where they sat on the coffin. He started to lash them with his whip, as the cart passed by, and ordered them to be silent. This they did, but on reaching the graveyard, they again took up their wailings, whereupon the priest forced them down from the coffin with his whip.[14]

Angela Bourke has suggested that Synge 'would have known something about the Irish practice of lamentation before he heard women in Aran give voice to it',[15] and proceeds to imply that the dramatist may have studied *caoineadh* in works such as Thomas Crofton Croker's *Researches in the South of Ireland*.[16] There is, however, no manuscript evidence to suggest that Synge read this work or, indeed, that the dramatist had ever encountered *caoineadh* before he arrived on Inis Meáin in May 1898, where he recorded:

---

[12] John McCarthy, 'The Famine in Cork, Clare and Waterford' Irish Folklore Commission Manuscript: 1071, f.276. County Roscommon. While McCarthy's folklore was recorded in County Roscommon, the family had moved there from Enniskean, County Cork.

[13] George Petrie, *The Petrie Collection of the Ancient Music of Ireland*, vol. 1 (Dublin: Dublin University Press, 1855), p. xii.

[14] Seán Ó Súilleabháin, *Irish Wake Amusements* (Cork: The Mercier Press, 1967), p. 143.

[15] Angela Bourke, 'Keening as Theatre: J.M. Synge and the Irish Lament Tradition' in Nicholas Grene, ed., *Interpreting Synge: Essays from the Synge Summer School, 1991-2000* (Dublin: Lilliput, 2000), p. 69.

[16] Bourke, 'Keening as Theatre' p. 69. Bourke argues that in 'the years before [Synge] began to make regular visits to the islands, Irish readers of English has been introduced to *caoineadh* as a source of romantic poetry. Thomas Crofton Croker's Researches in the South of Ireland (1824) and the Keen of the South of Ireland (1844) had drawn attention to the traditional oral lament many years before'.

> Each old woman, as she took her turn in the leading recitative, seemed possessed for the moment with a profound ecstasy of grief, swaying to and fro, and bending her forehead to the stone before her, while she called out to the dead with a perpetually recurring chant of sobs. All round the graveyard other wrinkled women, looking out from under the deep red petticoats that cloaked them, rocked themselves with the same rhythm, and intoned the inarticulate chant that is sustained by all as an accompaniment. [...] They [the women] are usually silent, but in the presence of death all outward show of indifference or patience is forgotten, and they shriek with pitiable despair before the horror of the fate to which they are all doomed. Before they covered the coffin an old man kneeled down by the grave and repeated a simple prayer for the dead. [...] There was an irony in these words of atonement and Catholic belief spoken by voices that were still hoarse with the cries of pagan desperation.[17]

Accordingly, the Synge scholar can only conclude that the dramatist, raised on the Protestant ethic of humility and the privatization of grief, must have been shocked when he first observed the howling and wailing that is concomitant with what he must have considered to be a pre-Christian ritual of Gothic excess.

By choosing to stage *caoineadh* in *Riders to the Sea*, Synge's injunction to Catholic Ireland was clear: watch a performance of the discontents of historical time, or else allow the progressive historicism of a modernizing Catholic Church turn collective memory into the fictions of history. To a man like Johnnie Synge, this smacked of wanton cultural imperialism. Synge's commitment to the staging of a volatile and veracious pre-Christian ritual was the dramatist's attempt to bring a named but unknowable pre-modern culture into Irish hegemonic cultural discourse that was determined by the politics of Catholic progressive modernity. Analysis of the dialectic between two temporalities (the modern and the pre-modern) and *caoineadh* moves discourse on *Riders to the Sea* (hereafter *Riders*) away from the cliché of cottage-kitchen realism and national identity politics, and towards an interrogation of the cultural hegemony of modernity and the discontents of historical time in *fin-de-siècle* Ireland.

The Discontents of Historical Time

Catholic Ireland deemed *caoineadh* pre-modern and pre-political because it was seemingly unable to adapt to the changes that had been made to religion, economics and politics, which had been implemented with Ireland's transition to capitalism in 1848; as Christina Brophy has suggested, 'in the mid-nineteenth century, the religious and cultural underpinnings of the *caoineadh* deteriorated due to opposition from strong farmers and clergy as well as the decimation of the rural labouring class'.[18] As Joseph Lee has suggested, these

---

17 Synge, *Collected Works*, vol. 2, *Prose*, pp. 74-5.

18 Christina S. Brophy, 'Keening Community: Mná Caointe, Women, Death and Power in Ireland' (PhD diss., Boston College, 2010), p. 5. Furthermore, Joseph Lee points out that the 'root of the problem in many backward economies lies in agriculture.

institutional changes witnessed the Catholic Church display 'an obsession with the materialists' as Catholic society displaced 'other worldly values' in favour of 'a very intense "this worldly" concern with social status'.[19] The privileging of economic capital predicated Catholic modernity, which, in turn, ensured that Catholic modernity remained 'politically pragmatic' as it attempted to 'foster a sense of national political consciousness'.[20] But the cultural residue from pre-Christian Ireland could not simply disappear, which is why it was perceived to inhabit the national-popular fantasy space as the consummation of the Celtic Geist, thus creating a curious paradox. Pre-Christian residual culture could be instrumental in the articulation of state-orientated nationalism. However, if the pre-Christian fantasy of the Celtic Geist materialized as pre-Christian reality then it was promptly removed from cultural hegemony, because its apparent pre-political logic was problematical for the habitations of Catholic, bourgeois modernity.

What is significant about the performance of *caoineadh* in *fin-de-siècle* Ireland is that as capitalism began to articulate Catholic modernity, members of the Irish populace still rationalized material conditions with pre-Christian sensibilities (such as *caoineadh*) which invited the contemporaneity of the pre-modern with the modern and the political with the pre-political. What emerges in this discrepancy between religious belief and political persuasion is the pluralization of modernity that demanded a heteroglossia of the political. For if the realm of the political was marked by the logic of Catholic modernity, then Synge's staging of *caoineadh* in *Riders to the Sea* is a performative heteroglossia; a staging of a pre-modern and pre-political sensibility in front of a predominantly Catholic audience whose ideological persuasion was significantly influenced by the Church.

Material conditions in Ireland necessarily changed under the impact of capitalism but what remained was the dominance of capitalism without the hegemony of a capitalist culture. If political power and economic capital are treated as two separate categories then the category of the political has the potential to be insurgent towards Catholic modernity because it is no longer oppressive but productive. In distancing itself from pre-Christian sensibilities, Catholic modernity only succeeded in enfranchising the cultural residue as a political power that pluralized modernity through the constellation of the pre-modern and the modern. Synge understood that *caoineadh* could not be regulated to a pre-modern and pre-political consciousness. Just because these sensibilities invited the concomitance of pre-capitalist modernity, it did not

---

Food supply is so low that a sufficient surplus to feed a substantial non-agricultural population cannot be generated. This was not the case in Ireland' (Joseph Lee, *The Modernisation of Irish Society: 1848-1918* [Dublin: Gill and Macmillan, 1989], p. 9). With the introduction of capitalism, Irish 'commercial farming had superseded subsistence agriculture over three-quarters of the country by 1850, when Ireland had one of the most commercially advanced agricultures in the world' (Lee, *The Modernisation of Irish Society*, p. 10).

[19] Lee, *The Modernisation of Irish Society*, p. 16.

[20] Lee, ibid, pp. 49, 57-58.

necessarily follow that those that believed in them engage within the realm of the political. Ostensibly for Synge, *caoineadh* was not the false consciousness of pre-modernity but the cultural articulation of a consciousness that precluded the institutional logic of Catholic, bourgeois modernity. At this juncture, the cultural performance of *caoineadh* is in itself a political act that necessitates an alternative temporality of modernity where the pre-modern and the modern are no longer incommensurable but inextricable.

Synge's dramatization of *caoineadh* in *Riders* warrants a cultural materialist reading of the historical record so that history can be brushed against the grain in Walter Benjamin's useful phrase.[21] To this end, Benjamin advocates that there 'is no document of civilization which is not at the same time a document of barbarism', that is to say civilizations regulate a punitive understanding of historical time and those documents (such as *caoineadh*) that do not harmoniously synthesize are left to stalk the corridors of the national subconscious.[22] For what Catholic hegemony in *fin-de-siècle* Ireland feared, most of all, was not a rationality that was heathen, but a rationality that operated in a differential temporality of modernity within the nation-state's hegemony; *caoineadh* is indexical of such rationality. If we accept that history cannot be defined by any temporal model (i.e. what survives from the past) then, all of a sudden, the historical record is necessarily dependent upon the logic of modernity to valorize its own articulation. With respect to a critique of progressive historicism, Dipesh Chakrabarty maintains that the historian must learn 'to think the present – the "now" that we inhabit as we speak – as irreducibly not-one'.[23] From this perspective, the fundamental disjuncture between the past and the present emerges at the interface of a progressive historicism, which results in an alternative temporality (the not-one) where the pre-modern lies cheek by jowl with the modern. *Caoineadh* occupies the temporal not-one. It is from this alternative understanding of temporality, modernity and its historical discontents that we can begin to move towards an understanding of how *caoineadh* pluralized Catholic Ireland's objective measurement of temporality.

Synge's engagement with *caoineadh* certainly follows suit with some of his fellow Anglo-Irish directors of the Abbey: W.B. Yeats, Lady Augusta Gregory. Indeed, in Joseph Holloway's diary it is possible to see a smudged footnote added after his initial entry where he reminds himself: 'I heard the "Riders to the Sea" "styled" the drama of the clique'.[24] *Riders* is certainly a drama of an esoteric clique that purloined pre-Christian cultural residue for aesthetic

---

21 Walter Benjamin, *Illuminations*, trans. Harry Zorn, ed. Hannah Arendt (London: Pimlico, 1999), p. 248.

22 Benjamin, *Illuminations*, p. 248.

23 Dipesh Chakrabarty, *Provincializing Europe: Postcolonial Thought and Historical Difference* (Princeton: Princeton University Press, 2000), p. 249.

24 Joseph Holloway, 25 February 1904. The National Library of Ireland Manuscript: 1802. *Impressions of A Dublin Playgoer*, vol. 1, *January-June 1904*, ff.95-96. Hereafter quoted as NLI MS: and folio number. All quotes comes with permission from the National Library of Ireland.

impulse, which is why Paul Murphy has correctly suggested that Synge follows suit with the 'Ascendancy trait of constructing the peasantry as fantasy objects, functioning as the key components in an ideological assault on bourgeois economics and a defence of aristocratic virtues.'[25] However, Synge's decision to stage *caoineadh* should be considered as an act of strategic essentialism that demonstrates his commitment to those cultural formations that were oppressed by the habitations of Catholic modernity. The salient analysis of Synge's recalcitrance to Catholic Ireland has been modelled by the academy as the materialization of Synge's wounded pride as the Anglo-Irish Ascendancy underwent a neurotic fall from grace in which the Irish peasantry occupy 'a fantasyscape that forms the metaphysical superstructure of Anglo-Irish ideology'.[26] But it is also true the dramatist had sincere problems with Catholic Ireland's totalizing narrative of historical progress. An alternative reading of Synge's engagement with the material conditions of the Irish peasantry is warranted.

After reading Karl Marx, Synge defined himself as 'a radical', making the conscious decision 'to change things root and branch'.[27] The dramatist had heeded Marx's dictum that maintained the ideology of a social formation was best analysed when it was still in the throes of enfranchisement; when those essential components had not yet been harmonized and/or masked. In the Irish context, Synge was able to consider the enfranchisement of the Catholic bourgeoisie with Marx's injunction in mind. What became evidently clear to Synge was the absence of those so-called embarrassing elements of Gaelic culture (such as *caoineadh*) that the bourgeoisie had suppressed in the wake of the Famine. By staging *caoineadh* in *Riders* Synge was, in essence, dramatizing an innate Gaelic culture that was neither imported, nor mummified by his Revivalist colleagues but rather, a living, breathing, subterranean culture that would construct a constellation of the pre-modern and the modern. As Benjamin points out, 'history is the subject of a structure whose site is not homogenous, empty time, but time filled by the presence of the now'.[28] But in Synge's Ireland, history as being in time (*Dasien*) was not the case, which is why the dramatist's seditious staging of the past would use cultural memory to puncture and punctuate progressive history. 'Without memory' Paul Ricouer has suggested, 'there is no principle of hope' and if 'we cease to believe that heritages from the past can yet be reinterpreted' then, in the final analysis, 'all historical mediation [has] become empty'.[29] The staging of *caoineadh*, then, is not simply an unethical, rearguard defence predicated on Anglo-Irish class

[25] Murphy, *Hegemony and Fantasy in Irish Drama*, 1899-1949, pp. 29-30.

[26] Murphy, ibid., p. 35.

[27] J.M. Synge, quoted in Edward M. Stephens, 'John Synge: manuscript of the biography of John Millington Synge by Edward M. Stephens' in The Stephens-Synge Manuscripts from the Library of Trinity College Dublin: 6193, f. 1663. This quote comes with permission from The Board of Trinity College.

[28] Benjamin, *Illuminations*, pp. 252-53.

[29] Paul Ricoeur, *Time and Narrative*, vol. 3, trans. Kathleen Blamey and David Pellauer (Chicago: Chicago University Press, 1988), p. 258.

insecurity, but a performance philosophy of modernity. And significantly, Synge's insistence on the pluralization of absolute time from the space and place of *Inis Meáin* had a provenance in scholarship: Celtology.

'Où les morts continuent une vie'[30]

In the decades before the Revival, European Celtologists had successfully laid to rest esoteric debates over the authenticity of a Celtic culture that saturated Revivalist discourse and Synge, who diligently attended Prof. Henri d'Arbois de Jubainville's lectures at the Sorbonne, had been a part of the debate. In the same year that Synge wrote *Riders to the Sea*, the dramatist published an article in *L'Européen* entitled 'La Vieille Littérature Irlandaise' in which he praised De Jubainville's knowledge of Celtic Ireland and proceeded to point out that:

> Rien, par exemple, dans la littérature n'est aussi primitif que cette foi commune aux Grecs et Irlandais, foi en un autre monde où les morts continuent une vie semblable à l'existence terrestre sans espoir d'être récompensés pour leurs vertus ni appréhension d'être punis pour leurs méfaits.
> [Nothing in literature, for example, is as primitive as this faith common to the Greeks and the Irish, faith in another world where the dead continue to live a life similar to earthly existence without hope either of being rewarded for their virtues or of being punished for their misdeeds.[31]]

Synge's knowledge of the pre-Christian Otherworld was predicated upon his reading of *The Voyage of Bran* and within his detailed notes from reading that text, the dramatist wrote himself a reminder: 'Observe that the idea of Hell absent from primitive texts gradually assumes such prominence that it at last completely overshadows the idea of heaven. In Irish and non-Christian texts no hell'.[32]Anthony Roche maintains that 'unlike Christian notions of an otherworld, this Elysium is on and of the earth and its rewards are depicted very much in terms of the natural and man-made world.'[33] In his notebook Synge continued his ruminations on the Otherworld by reminding himself that 'Irish and Hellenic alone preserved the first stage of the otherworld conception which is solely gods' land unconnected with man's fate'.[34] In *Riders* Maurya's *caoine* makes reference to neither heaven nor hell because *caoineadh* was concomitant with the Otherworld; to permeate this pre-Christian belief with Catholic beliefs would only fly in the face of Synge's studies on the Otherworld that he had learnt from *The Voyage of Bran*, from which he made the following conclusion: 'The Celtic Doctrine of Re-Birth [is a] pre-Christian Irish Otherworld vision [that] finds its closest analogues in the earliest known stage

---

[30] Synge, *Collected Works*, vol. 2, *Prose*, p. 354.
[31] Ibid.
[32] TCD MS: 4378, f.49v.
[33] Anthony Valentine Roche, 'The Otherworld Drama of John Millington Synge' (PhD diss., The University of California: Santa Barbara, 1984), p. vii.
[34] TCD MS: 4378, f.49v.

of Hellenic belief and forms with them the most archaic Aryan presentiment of the divine happy land.'[35] In *Riders*, then, Bartley has not passed into heaven or hell but, just like his elder brother, he continues to live in eternal youth in the *Tír na nÓg* (Land of the Young). And just how Bartley gets there is necessarily determined by the relativity of space and time that Synge encountered on *Inis Meáin*, where the islanders did not make a 'distinction between the natural and the supernatural'.[36]

Caoineadh collapses time into a tripartite structure where past events are summoned in the present in order to facilitate future life. The magical intervention on behalf of the deceased in order to ensure a safe passage to the Otherworld is the primary function of *caoineadh*, rather than a cathartic expression of grief. Breandán Ó Madagáin advocates that the *caoine* primarily held a 'supernatural ritual function: to transfer the spirit of the deceased from this world to that of the spirits'.[37] Bourke points out that the *ban caointhe* would ensure that 'most of the lament is an address to the corpse, she speaks not to the dead but to the living, and to the recently dead person as a member of the community of those living, but one who is about to defect.'[38] The *ban caointhe* does this because she considers the deceased to be present within the community as a supernatural phenomenon that requires help to be transported to the Otherworld.

The plurality of absolute time where the living can orchestrate the passage of the living-dead to the Otherworld was why Edmund Spenser found the performance particularly disturbing, because it offered 'no hope of [Christian] salvation'.[39] Hence why the Church was so hostile towards *caoineadh*, because it was not compatible with Catholic doctrine. Heated exchanges between the *ban caointhe* and the Church were commonplace; a woman who was advised by her parish priest to cease her *caoine* was said to have replied: '*Éist, a Shagairt agus seasuigh díreach, Léigh an tAifreann is gheobhaidh tú díol as*. (Shut up, Priest, and stand up straight! Read the Mass and you'll get paid!).[40] Traditionally the *ban caointhe* would have never laced her performance with seditious stabs at the Church but rather, her performance would involve a codified discourse on communal politics; from problems in marital relations to communal strife. But Maurya's *caoine* is far more provocative because it is a codified rhetoric of resistance against the Catholic Church:

---

[35] TCD MS: 4378, f.49r.

[36] Synge, *Collected Works*, vol. 2, *Prose*, p. 75.

[37] Breandán Ó Madagáin, *Caointe Agus Seancheolta Eile: Keening and Other Old Irish Musics* (Indreabhán, Conamara: Cló Iar-Chonnachta, 2005), p. 81.

[38] Angela Bourke, "The Irish Traditional Lament and the Grieving Process," *Women's Studies International Forum, Special Issue: Feminism in Ireland* 11, no. 4 (1988): pp. 289-90.

[39] Edmund Spenser, *Ireland under Elizabeth and James The First, Described by Edmund Spenser, by Sir John Davis and Fynes Moryson*, ed. Henry Morley (London: George Routledge and Sons, 1890), pp. 95, 94.

[40] Angela Bourke, 'More in Anger than in Sorrow: Irish Women's Lament Poetry' in Joan Newlon Radner, ed. *Feminist Messages: Coding in Women's Folk Culture* (Urbana: University of Illinois Press, 1993), p. 167.

> They're all together this time, and the end is come. May The Almighty God have mercy on Bartley's soul, and on Michael's soul, and on the souls of Sheamus and Patch, and Stephen and Shawn [*bending her head*] ... and, may He have mercy on my soul, Nora, and on the soul of every one is left living in the world. [*She pauses, and the keen rises a little more loudly from the women, then sinks away. Continuing.*] Michael has a clean burial in the far north, by the grace of the Almighty God. Bartley will have a fine coffin out of the white boards, and a deep grave surely. What more can we want than that? No man at all can be living for ever, and we must be satisfied.[41]

In her *caoine* Maurya bypasses communal politicking and directs a formulaic rhetoric of resistance directly against the Catholic Church by failing to predicate her *caoine* on any Catholic eschatology. Returning to Synge's notebook, it is possible to see that Synge thought that 'Irish and Hellenic alone preserved the first stage of the otherworld conception ~~that~~ which it is [sic] solely god's land unconnected with man's fate'[42] and that the Otherworld was always 'framed without reference to man's future life'[43] and this is precisely why Maurya's *caoine* is not indexical of either divine reward or punishment, simply because Synge understood Heaven and Hell to be impositions on the Celtic concept of the Otherworld. This is why the *Freeman's Journal* took issue with Maurya's *caoine,* because they believed that 'her prayers to Providence may cease, [and she] leaves off her praying just when Irish peasant's prayers would really begin.'[44] In short, Synge knew 'nothing of Irish peasant religion'.[45] However, Maurya does not need to pray for the divine entrance of her sons into Heaven because, as Synge recorded from Celtology, entrance to the Otherworld is always 'dissociated from eschatological belief'.[46]

By staging the performance of Maurya's *caoine* in accordance with Celtology, not only was Synge dramatizing the rhetoric of resistance that necessarily permeates *caoineadh*, he was, in the final analysis, sanctioned by Celtology to use the discontents of historical time to critique Catholic progressive historicism's orthodox measurement of absolute time. The peasantry in Synge's *Riders* may be indicative of an Anglo-Irish fantasyscape, but their cultural practises were far from fantastical. And so, as *Riders* went into performance the pre-Christian fantasy became an alarming reality.

Perform, or Else!

As Joseph Holloway stepped out of Molesworth Hall into Dublin's February night air, he knew something was wrong. Holloway had just attended the premier of *Riders to the Sea* (1904), a production that J.M. Synge directed.

---

41 Synge, *Collected Works*, vol. 3, *Plays*, pp. 26-27.
42 TCD MS: 4378, f.49v.
43 TCD MS: 4378, f.49v.
44 Anonymous, 'Irish National Theatre: Mr. Synge's New Play' *The Freeman's Journal*, 6 February 1905.
45 Ibid.
46 TCD MS: 4378, f.49v.

Synge just about managed to attend the premier because, as Mrs Synge recorded in her diary, her son was suffering acute pain from an abscessed tooth, which was accompanied by a high temperature; certainly for the rest of the run 'Johnnie [was] very poorly with abscess in his face, staid in bed [sic]'.[47] It was probably a good thing that Synge remained absent. The last play of Synge's that Holloway saw, *The Shadow of the Glen* (1903), centred on a wake, and *Riders to the Sea* the dramatist's next play, centred upon another pre-Christian death ritual: the *caoine*. Familiar with jingoistic drama, Holloway could hardly believe his eyes. Arriving home to 21 Northumberland Street, the architect-cum-theatre-critic fumbled for his diary:

> Before a very distinguished audience the National Theatre Society presented JM Synge's intensely sad sketch of fisher-life on an island off the west coast of Ireland [...] The entrance of the keeners...was nearly proving fatal to the solemnity of the situation, but luckily they did not.[48]

Holloway was used to the dramatization of pre-Christian Ireland, but it was always hermetically sealed within the ancient-saga texts and those 'historical plays' that Lady Gregory believed to be absolutely necessary to 'take a grip of the people'.[49] To radically deviate from an absolute measurement of time that was not co-dependent on those spaces and places of supposedly forgotten time (*Inis Meáin*), as Synge had chosen to do, was to postulate an alliance between a subterranean culture of pre-Christianity and the Catholic nation-state. Such sedition called into question the orthodoxy of the Irish postcolonial project; why should Irish independence be granted if the populace are saturated with pre-Christian heathens? Indeed, the British Empire had perennially considered *caoineadh* to be indicative of a backward, pre-modern and pre-political Irish consciousness. In Ireland the Elizabethan poet, Edmund Spenser, stumbled across 'lewd crying and howling' and considered the *caoine* to be indexical of 'Sycthian barbarism', because it was 'altogether heathenish'.[50] While touring Ireland in the middle of the nineteenth century, Mr and Mrs S.C. Hall watched a performance of *caoineadh*. So alarmed were they that, upon returning to Britain, they consulted the Rev G.N. Wright, who informed them that such a savage practice 'was of very ancient date, and can be traced back to heathen origin with tolerable certainty.'[51]

Synge had intended that there were to be 'no fake about the show'.[52] The critic from the *Irish Times* was struck by Synge's realism: 'the long exposure of the dead body before an audience may be realistic, but it certainly is not

---

47 Kathleen Synge, 26 February 1904. *The Stephens-Synge Manuscripts from the Library of Trinity College Dublin*: 6219, f. 67. This quote comes with permission from The Board of Trinity College, Dublin.

48 NLI MS: 1802, f.95n.

49 NYPL MS: 65b2290, ff.29-30.

50 Spenser, *Ireland under Elizabeth and James The First*, p. 95.

51 Mr and Mrs S.C. Hall, *Ireland: Its Scenery, Character, &c*, vol. 1 (London: How and Parsons, 1841), pp. 222n-23n.

52 Synge, *Collected Works*, vol. 3, *Plays*, p. xix.

artistic. There are some things which are lifelike, and yet are quite unfit for presentation on the stage[,] and *Riders to the Sea* is one of them.'[53] The style of *caoineadh* that Synge mobilizes in *Riders* requires the actor playing Maurya to deliver the *caoine* in an extempore fashion. In the years after Synge's death, the Abbey actor George Roberts criticized the directors for allowing 'too much "composition" about the *caoine* in the Abbey in later years, and too little of the passionate sorrow which should inform it.'[54] The efficacy of *caoineadh*, then, required the performer to become lost, Shaman-like, in a ritual performance of grief. This required considerable dedication and skill from the actor, and this is why Synge drafted in a *ban caointhe* (female keener) from Galway who lived in a decaying tenement just off Gardiner Street, Dublin, to teach the precise schematics of the *caoine* to the company. The lady was actually discovered by Roberts, and his account of the ritual performance of the *caoine* is indexical of how Synge thought the *caoine* in *Riders* should be performed:

> Synge was exceedingly anxious that 'caoine' should be as close as possible to the peculiar chant that is used in the islands, and after much searching I found a Galway woman living in one of the Dublin suburbs who consented to show two of the girls how the caoine was given. [...] She was very interested in the whole affair, wanting to know what the play was about, and saying the caoine was so terrible a thing she could hardly believe people would want to put it in a play. [...] She lighted the wake candles, and then she got that note full of terror of the dead. [...] She was a native Irish speaker, and the Irish cadences and rhythm of the words, in conjunction with the clapping of the hands and swaying of her body, made a scene very terrible and yet beautiful to look on.[55]

The actress, Máire Nic Shiubhlaigh (one of the girls that Roberts identifies) would later recall the precise nature of the lady's *caoine*:

> swaying backwards and forwards with the rise and fall of the music [...] It was strangely moving to see this old figure standing at the window of a crumbling tenement, looking over a city street singing. She seemed to forget we were there. She sang: "*Tà sé imighthe uaim*! *Go deo*! *Go deo*! *Go deo*!"[56*] [...] They were thin, piping notes [...] The *caoin* [sic] seemed to possess her. Synge might have written this play around her alone; an old woman counting the loss of her sons with a bitter satisfaction.[57]

On the following night Holloway returned to the theatre for the second performance of *Riders*. Upon returning home that evening he sat at his writing table and concluded his performance analysis of *caoineadh* in *Riders*:

---

[53] Anonymous, 'Irish National Theatre Society' *The Irish Times*, 26 February 1904.

[54] George Roberts, 'Memoirs of George Roberts', *The Irish Times*, 2 August 1955.

[55] Roberts, 'Memoirs of George Roberts', 2 August 1955.

[56] Máire Nic Shiubhlaigh, *The Splendid Years: Recollections of Maire Nic Shiubhlaigh, as told to Edward Kenny* 'He is gone from me! Forever! Forever! Forever!' (Dublin: James Duffy, 1955), p. 55.

> I have come to the conclusion that a more gruesome ... play than *Riders to the Sea* has seldom if ever been staged before. The thoroughly in earnest playing of the company made the terribly depressing "wake" episode so realistic ... that some of the audience could not stand the painful horror of the scene, & had to leave the hall during its progress.[58]

Synge had succeeded in contesting the hegemony of dominant Catholic specularity by bringing on stage that which was, at once, anathema to modernity and the fulcrum upon which a modernist aesthetic could be balanced. Significantly, Holloway and his fellow spectators who interrogated the temporality of the pre-modern stage-picture were unable to coalesce with Synge's modernist aesthetic simply because the specularity of the pre-modern punctuated the cultural analysis of the Catholic populace. And so, Synge's spectators were forced to leave the theatre because they could not reconcile the barbarism of a pre-Christian ritual performance under the auspices of aesthetic efficacy, let alone under the auspices of forgotten history. In London Max Beerbohm, upon leaving the premiere of *Riders*, was delighted by the performance of *caoineadh* and in the *Saturday Review* he wrote that the *caoine* had an 'utter incapacity to be vulgar' and concluded by saying: 'I delight in the recollection of it as it was. And still cherished in my ears are the soft echoes.'[59] But back in Dublin such was the dominance of Catholic specularity that Synge's mirror was shattered. Arthur Clery (James Joyce's classmate at University College Dublin), who wrote under the name of 'Chanel' failed to stomach the 'distraught wailings of an Arran mother [...] [which is] horribly depicted, the caóin forming [...] a dire obligation to her murmurings'.[60]

With respect to *caoineadh*, David Lloyd has argued that 'if the sound is quite literally haunting, that is surely because it picks up and foregrounds a whole chain of representations of the Famine and its psychological effects that recur through virtually every account, journalistic, historical and fictional'.[61] It is because the dead were not properly venerated during the Famine that they were left to stalk the melancholic corridors of the cultural consciousness where they reappeared, as the repressed must, unexpectedly but nevertheless poignantly within the temporality of the present: Synge's dramatization of caoineadh in *Riders*. From this perspective, in performance, *caoineadh* extends further than Maurya's desperation for the loss of her family and can be considered to be a startling and shocking performance of the pre-modern within the modern, rather than a simple fetishization *qua* Anglo-Irish fantasyscape.

---

[58] NLI MS: 1802, f.99.

[59] Max Beerbohm, 'Some Irish Plays and Players', *Saturday Review*, 9 April 1904.

[60] Chanel, 'The National Theatre', *Leader*, 5 March 1904.

[61] David Lloyd, 'The Memory of Hunger' in David L. Eng and David Kazanijan, eds., *Loss: The Politics of Mourning* (Berkeley: University of California Press, 2003), pp. 205-06.

'Acting in the direction of the future'[62]

Before writing *Riders* Synge drafted an essay entitled 'Historical and Peasant Drama'. In one draft of the essay Synge concluded that when 'the sense of historical truth awakes in Europe[,] historical fiction becomes impossible'.[63] This is why his dramaturgical praxis summons the contemporaneity of the dead in order to use the discontents of history to contest the dominant specularity of the cultural text. For if progressive historicism buries the dead but perennially mourns their passing, then the discontents of historical time (*caoineadh*) does not allow the dead to rest, but authenticates the repertoire to ghost the archive. The performance of *caoineadh* in *Riders* is one of the repertoire because, as Diana Taylor reminds us, the repertoire 'enacts embodied memory: performances, gestures, orality, movement, dance, singing – in short, all those acts usually thought of as ephemeral, non-reproducible knowledge', and significantly, a performance of the repertoire 'allows for an alternative perspective on historical processes'.[64] The *caoine* in *Riders* had the historiographical potential to be insurgent against the archive, thus pluralizing the historical authenticity of Catholic progressive historicism.

In *Riders* Synge disavows the therapy of mourning, literally, *caoineadh* for the dead, because the dead are concomitant with a tripartite temporal structure, which is why Maurya maintains that 'they're altogether this time'.[65] Synge was before his time by realizing that if the past can crystallize in the present then it will allow the nation-state to remember the future. As Heidegger has suggested, 'it is remarkable how, in acting in the direction of the future, the past comes alive and the present vanishes. Those who act authentically live from out of the future and also can live from out of the past; the present takes care of itself.'[66] Synge allowed his spectator to be in time with the performance of *caoineadh*, quite literally the spectator had to be there (*Dasein*) in order to feel and subsequently testify the affective power of a performance of cultural memory. And so if, at the beginning of his career, Synge defined himself as 'a radical' who would 'change things root and branch', there is certain pathos in John Butler Yeats's epitaph, scribbled in his diary at the Grand Nassau Hotel, Dublin, after Synge's premature passing on 24 March 1909: 'cut is the branch that might have grown full and straight'.[67]

CHRISTOPHER COLLINS teaches at the Department of Drama, Trinity College Dublin and at the Lir: The National Academy of Dramatic Art. A Trinity College

62 Heidegger, *Supplements*, p. 169.

63 TCD MS 4396, 61r.

64 Diana Taylor, *The Archive and the Repertoire: Performing Cultural Memory in the Americas* (Durham: Duke University Press, 2003), p. 20.

65 Synge, *Collected Works*, vol. 3, *Plays*, p. 27.

66 Heidegger, *Supplements*, p. 169.

67 John Butler Yeats, 'John Synge is Dead' in *Foster-Murphy Collection. Manuscripts and Archives Division, The New York Public Library, Astor, Lenox and Tilden Foundations* MS: Holo. 850. & TS signed, f.3. This quote comes with permission from The New York Public Library.

Dublin Gold Medalist, he completed his PhD at Trinity in 2012, winning the Irish Society for Theatre Research's New Scholar's Prize in the same year. He has published widely on Synge's collected works and, with Mary P. Caulfield he has co-edited a collection of essays entitled *Ireland, Memory and Performing the Historical Imagination* that is being published by Palgrave Macmillan. He also works professionally as a dramaturg, director and an Applied Theatre practitioner.

Scenographic Interactions: 1950s' Ireland and Dublin's Pike Theatre

SIOBHÁN O'GORMAN

[The limits of scenography – like the limits of performance – are being continually expanded so that it is no longer contained within the theatre but can refer to the performative environments beyond. In this context, Ireland of the 1950s can be seen to have undergone significant scenographic changes, in which visual culture was harnessed to improve Ireland's performance on the international stage. This essay engages both established and emerging definitions of scenography. It explores how the pioneering work of the Pike theatre, Dublin, can be seen to endorse a 'stage of re-vision' within Irish theatre of the 1950s. However, I also examine the ways in which the Pike's scenographic aesthetics interact complexly with the changing scenography of Ireland at large. In doing so, I aim to illuminate the ways in which Ireland's increasingly image-conscious culture can be seen to impact on the visual and performative character of Irish theatre.]

Introduction

In 1949, Ireland moved out of the British Commonwealth to become an independent republic. The following decade was characterized by ideological conflict: while conservative Catholic patriarchy continued to be reinforced top-down through state policy, Ireland's political establishment also instigated efforts to modernize and internationalize Ireland. The prospect of change was met with resistance from those espousing more traditional nationalist ideals based on cultural and economic isolationism. From 1958, the government's implementation of its Programmes for Economic Expansion consolidated the shift to an export-driven, inward capital investment economy. However, this state drive towards furthering Ireland's positioning within an internationalized modernity had already been underway from the late 1940s. The interactions of design, performance and space were key to these efforts, as exemplified in the formation of several outward-looking initiatives including the Irish Arts Council in 1951, Córas Tráchtála (the export board) in 1952, An Tóstal (a series of festivals celebrating Irish culture) in 1953, Bord Fáilte (the tourist board) in 1955 and the Dublin Theatre Festival in 1957. These organizations harnessed visual and theatrical culture to enhance Ireland's performance on the international stage, and to promote what can now be seen as a revisionist questioning of established national constructions.

Considering these developments, Ireland of the 1950s can be conceptualized both *at* (temporally) and *as* (performatively) a 'stage of re-vision' – a word that I hyphenate because Ireland's performance of revision is often played out at the level of visual culture. This involved a kindling of industrial design, advertising, public art, crafts, the fashion industry, theatre, pageants and festivals. Shannon Jackson's claim that 'visual culture seems to require performance for its seeing to be shown' elucidates my conception of 1950s' Ireland as 'a stage of re-vision'.[1]

Within the initiatives described above, aspects of the broad disciplines of performance studies (encompassing theatrical, cultural and economic performance) and visual culture can be seen to interact. Jackson offers a comparative analysis of these contemporaneous fields, arguing that this 'provides a way of foregrounding the stakes and obstacles faced in their shared consolidation'.[2] Building on Jackson's insightful comparisons, my interpretation situates scenography at the *interface* between performance studies and visual culture.

Scenography has traditionally been associated with scenic and atmospheric design for theatre productions. However, its remit has undergone an expansion in line with the turn to 'performance' in cultural studies. The limits of scenography – like the limits of performance – are being continually extended. Scenography is no longer contained within the theatre but can refer to the environment beyond it. This comprises a landscape with structures and décor of varying levels of permanence, impacted on by the actions of those who pass through it, and permeated by politics. Introducing a special issue of the journal *Performance Research* entitled 'On Scenography' in 2013, editors Sodja Lotker and Richard Gough use definitions that reflect the plurality of contemporary scenographic theory:

> They [scenographies] are framed and designated – places, series of spaces, points of perspective, ways of looking and routes that provide points of view, frames of vision and vantage points to look from. [...] The looking happens with the whole body, the movement through space and the kinaesthetic experience of space together with a sense of movement inside oneself as an experience of the scenographic.[3]

Scenography, whether within or beyond the theatre, may also be seen as a collaborative *doing* that incorporates diverse contributions: it is both kinetic and kinaesthetic. The publication of a *Performance Research* special issue on

---

1 Shannon Jackson, 'Performing Show and Tell: Disciplines of Visual Culture and Performance Studies', *Journal of Visual Culture*, 4 (2005), p. 164.

2 Ibid.

3 Sodja Lotker and Richard Gough, 'On Scenography: Editorial', *Performance Research*, 18.3 (2013), (pp. 4-5).

scenography, in addition to the recent emergence of international journals dedicated exclusively to the discipline including *Scene* and *Theatre Arts Journal*, evidences the 'research and creative endeavour that is being pursued to advance its purview, reach and application within and beyond theatre and performance design'.[4]

Understood in these broader ways, scenography becomes a useful theoretical framework for examining Irish cultural change during the 1950s. The present article discusses aspects of Ireland's scenographic histories, locating the Pike theatre, founded in Dublin in 1953, within contemporaneous shifts in Ireland's visual-performative ethos. I engage with more established as well as emerging applications of scenography to survey the drive towards design innovation that characterized 1950s' Ireland, in addition to issues concerning space and design at the Pike theatre specifically. Considering the Pike's inventive approaches in these areas, it can be situated within wider concerns with the performance of visual culture. Indeed, by regularly producing challenging plays from abroad, this theatre club has often been seen to support aspects of the state's modernizing agenda. Additionally, the frame of scenography reveals collaborative working processes as active in the innovation offered by the Pike. The club's pioneering work arguably promoted a 'stage of re-vision' within Irish theatre. However, in the Pike's scenographic interactions with the wider culture, it also can be seen – somewhat paradoxically – to interrogate the concurrent commodification of visual culture in Ireland. To explore these connections and tensions, I will start by outlining shifts in Ireland's wider cultural scenography pertinent to the Pike's era; then I will move on to analyse the interactions of space, design and performance at the Pike theatre itself; finally, I will examine the scenographic interrelationships of theatre and culture. In doing so, I hope to shed light on how Ireland's increasingly image-conscious values can be seen to impact on the visual and performative character of Irish theatre.

Ireland's Shifting Scenographies

Ireland's emergence as (and at) a 'stage of re-vision' during the 1950s was motivated by governmental objectives for improved economic performance on the wider world stage. Jon McKenzie's seminal book, *Perform or Else: From Discipline to Performance* (2001) seeks to theorize the interconnections of organizational, technological and cultural performance by arguing that 'performance' in its various guises can take on a Foucaultian disciplining in the context of globalization. McKenzie argues, for example, that the employee-assessment model of 'performance management', which has proliferated since the end of the Second World War, 'attunes itself to economic processes that are increasingly [...] globally oriented'.[5] While some argue that McKenzie's overall thesis self-consciously fails, claims such as the above can illuminate changing

[4] Lotker and Gough, p. 6.

[5] Jon McKenzie, *Perform or Else: From Discipline to Performance* (New York: Routledge, 2001), p. 6.

attitudes towards design and visual culture within Ireland's political establishment from the late 1940s on.[6] Diarmaid Ferriter, drawing on Bernadette Whelan, contends that:

> [S]tatistical reviews and planning exercises which were a compulsory part of the process of the European Recovery Programme [1948] and the Organisation for European Economic Co-operation [also 1948] exposed fundamental weaknesses of the economy and forced economists into making comparative analyses with other countries that were out-performing Ireland'.[7]

Transnational economic comparisons also impacted on Irish creative and cultural activities, which were increasingly valued for their international competitiveness, leading to ideals of 'artrepreneurship' disseminated mainly through developing tourism and export industries.[8] The Irish Arts Council, for example, was set up in response to Thomas Bodkin's *Report on the Arts in Ireland* (1949). Bodkin, former director of the National Gallery of Ireland, was at the time manager of the Barber Institute, Birmingham. The Department of Industry and Commerce of Ireland's first coalition government (1948-51) commissioned Bodkin's report, insisting that it assess industrial design as part of its remit. In response to the department's commercial agenda, Bodkin judged that there 'never has been a sustained alliance between the arts and industry in Ireland; and little has been done in the last fifty years to promote such a desirable aim'.[9]

The report was the first of many initiatives that could be seen to push a 'performance management' agenda in relation to Irish visual culture. The Arts Council incorporated the promotion of industrial design as part of its aims and sponsored the International Design Exhibition in 1954 with a view to impressing upon Irish people 'the vital importance of attractive craftsmanship in our industrial products [...] because without it our exports cannot compete in

---

[6] See Henry M. Sayer, 'Review of *Perform or Else: From Discipline to Performance*', *Modernism/modernity*, 10.1 (2003), 200-02. Sayer asserts 'the disintegration of the page as a tool of communication at book's end suggests that McKenzie understands all too well that his argument has ultimately crashed and burned. But he gives us much to think about along the way' (p. 201).

[7] Diarmaid Ferriter, *The Transformation of Ireland, 1900-2000* (London: Profile, 2004), p. 468. According to Ferriter, during the 1950s, Ireland had 'been forced to begin to see itself in the context of its relationship with its European neighbours, particularly regarding Marshall Aid funding from the United States and the beginnings of European post-war reconstruction. [...] The Marshall Aid period was significant in that it focused much attention on the difficulties of directing the economy away from protection towards more openness' (p. 467).

[8] Jen Harvie, *Fair Play: Art, Performance and Neoliberalism* (Basingstoke: Palgrave Macmillan, 2013), pp. 62-107. Here I am paraphrasing Harvie's terminology in Chapter 2, which is titled 'The Artrepreneur: Artists and Entrepreneurialism.' While Harvie's book focuses on arts practice and funding in Britain – and particularly London – from the 1990s on, I see her useful term 'artrepreneur' as having wider historical and geographical relevance.

[9] Thomas Bodkin, *Report on the Arts in Ireland* (Dublin: The Stationary Office, 1949), p. 36.

world markets'.[10] Following this, the 1956 Irish Design Exhibition toured the major urban centres of each province, presenting the work of leading Irish designers and design-conscious industries. Each exhibition was produced by the Design Research Unit of Ireland (established by the Arts Council) with prominent British design theorist, Misha Black, as consultant. Throughout the 1950s, a range of developments pushed visual culture to the forefront of modernization, industrialization and internationalization. Signa Design Consultants was founded by architect Michael Scott and visual artist Louis Le Brocquy in 1954. There were efforts to invigorate the fashion industry headed by London-trained Sybil Connelly, and to revitalize craft-training for industry at the National College of Art in Dublin. A group of Dutch graphic designers began to work in Ireland. First commissioned by Aer Lingus in 1951, they went on to implement their Bauhaus principles in other Irish advertising projects. One of these graphic artists, Guss Melai, for example, designed the harp symbol for the first Tóstal festival in 1953. By 1959, An Córas Tráchtála had taken over responsibility for design promotion with its leader, William H. Walsh, commissioning in 1961 'a panel of distinguished Scandinavian designers [to] visit Ireland to advise on what had to be done'.[11] As such, Walsh and his international allies were instrumental in engineering what has been termed the 'Irish Design Reform Movement of the 1960s'.[12]

The above discussed shifts in cultural and political attitudes also contributed to an alteration of urban landscapes, particularly Dublin. While Dublin retained much of its elegant Georgian and Victorian buildings throughout the 1950s, the advent of more minimalist, modernist aesthetics was evident in public advertising through billboards as well as advertisements and signage in shops and offices.[13] The RTÉ documentary, *In Flags or Flitters: Pictures of Dublin*, originally broadcast in 1991, showcases changes in the cultural and physical landscape of Ireland's capital city from the 1950s on, illuminating what could be referred to as the shifting scenography of Dublin city. It includes such images as Nelson's Pillar, which visitors paid money to climb during the 1950s, but which was demolished by an IRA bomb in 1966, as well as the transformation of O'Connell Street into 'a honky-tonk freeway' of commercial outlets, modernist office blocks and derelict sites between 1965 and 1985.[14]

Cities, their architecture and broader performative activities have entered the discourse of scenography, and currently proliferating theatre forms such as site-specific work and promenade pieces often harness the scenographic potential of urban spaces. To return to 1950s' Ireland, An Tóstal also allows us

[10] P.J. Little qtd. in Arts Council of Ireland and Design Research Unit of Ireland, *International Design Exhibition 1954* (Dublin: Hobson Morris, 1954), p. 3.

[11] John Turpin, 'The Irish Design Reform Movement of the 1960s', *Design Issues*, 3:1 (1986), p. 11.

[12] For more on the initiatives outlined in this paragraph, as well as the background and processes of Irish design reform, see Turpin's 'The Irish Design Reform Movement of the 1960s'.

[13] Turpin, pp. 5, 9.

[14] *In Flags or Flitters*, RTE, 1991, http://www.youtube.com/watch?v=glhlTizC53o [accessed 3 January 2014].

to look at urban space through the lens of scenography. This series of festivals, which took place between 1953 and 1958, had Dublin city decked out with public art and decorative structures as part of the events, and 'featured historico-religious spectacles with a strong patriotic flavour'.[15] With its nation-branding pageantry, An Tóstal had an agenda comparable to 'The Gathering 2013' – a series of Irish occasions and festivals held throughout the year aiming to celebrate Irish culture and to attract visitors including tourists and the Irish diaspora. Similarly, An Tóstal sought to promote Ireland as a tourist destination, as well as to entice the return of Irish emigrants.

Ireland's post-Second World War drive towards internationalized modernity would gain momentum in the decades leading up to the 'Celtic Tiger' era (which took place approximately between 1994 and 2008), but it was only nascent in the 1950s.[16] As such, during the 1950s, the desire to progress towards international economic competitiveness was kept in check by anxieties concerning the sociocultural consequences of modernization. Ernest Blythe's policies as managing director of the Abbey theatre between 1941 and 1967 can be seen in some ways to epitomize the struggle to maintain an established national identity. Contemporaries such as Tomás Mac Anna defend Blythe's role as managing director, arguing that he kept the Abbey afloat during the commercially difficult periods of 'Emergency' (Ireland's terminology for the Second World War, used to reflect the country's neutrality) and recession, as well as after the original theatre building and much of its equipment were destroyed by a fire in 1951.[17] More recent scholarship has contended that the period of Blythe's reign, due to his championing of theatre that showcased 'representative nationalism'[18] and 'the values of a rural, Catholic Ireland, as interpreted by Fianna Fáil',[19] was a rather stale one for the Abbey.[20] Meanwhile, from the 1940s on, small theatre companies emerged including Globe, Studio,

---

[15] Joan FitzPatrick Dean, *Riot and Great Anger: Stage Censorship in Twentieth-Century Ireland* (Madison: University of Wisconsin Press, 2004), p. 154.

[16] Patrick Lonergan, *Theatre and Globalization: Irish Drama in the Celtic Tiger Era* (Basingstoke: Palgrave Macmillan, 2009). In this seminal study, Lonergan examines how the Celtic Tiger period of rapid social change, unprecedented economic growth and heightened internationalization impacted on the Irish theatre industry, with a particular focus on the ways in which are Irish productions were presented and marketed abroad.

[17] Tomás Mac Anna, 'Ernest Blythe and the Abbey', in E.H. Mikhail, ed., *The Abbey Theatre: Interviews and Recollections* (Totowa, New Jersey: Barnes and Noble, 1988), pp. 167-72.

[18] Lionel Pilkington, 'Theatre, Sexuality and State: Tennessee Williams's *The Rose Tattoo* at the Dublin Theatre Festival, 1957' in Nicholas Grene and Patrick Lonergan, eds., *Interactions: Dublin Theatre Festival 1957-2007* (Dublin: Carysfort Press, 2008), p. 24.

[19] Mary Trotter, *Modern Irish Theatre* (Cambridge: Polity, 2008), p. 119.

[20] See also Christopher Morash, *A History of Irish Theatre, 1601-2000* (Cambridge: Cambridge University Press, 2002), p. 212. Here, Morash outlines critical responses indicating that theatre presented by the Abbey during this period was often perceived as dull compared with alternative theatre productions. From this perspective he contends, for example, that the 'excitement generated by [...] amateur productions was in sharp contrast to the boredom of which Abbey audiences so often complained'.

37 Club, Pike, Orion and Gemini. These offered alternatives to the seemingly tired images of Irishness played out on the Abbey's national stage.

The Pike Theatre: Space, Design and Innovation

From the above list of emergent companies, the Pike is best remembered for making controversial interventions in Irish theatre of the 1950s, particularly in relation to its 1957 production of Tennessee Williams' *The Rose Tattoo*, which had opened on Broadway in 1951 and was released as a film adaptation in 1955. The Pike's production, charged with indecency and profanity, famously led to the arrest of Pike co-founder, Alan Simpson and – eventually, due to legal costs and a lapse in public support – contributed to the demise of this important theatre club. The Pike aimed to become, and succeeded in becoming, a revolutionary force in Irish theatre and can be seen as part of 'a "new wave" of theatrical experimentation that was also taking place in London and Paris.'[21] The club appeared to covet controversy in its efforts to 'stir up the theatrical lethargy of post-war Ireland'.[22] This is evidenced by its performative image both on and off-stage: the Pike supported the work of those who, at the time, could be seen as national and Abbey exiles (Samuel Beckett and Brendan Behan respectively);[23] several of its productions seemed almost to fetishize foreignness and, as Lionel Pilkington has rightly argued, heterosexual bodies;[24] meanwhile, the club is simultaneously remembered for hosting decadent parties.[25] Within a nation struggling to emerge from sexual repression and cultural isolationism, the Pike certainly appears as 'a cultural phenomenon that celebrated the arrival of a new, urban, liberal elite and a social space in which audience members could perform with brio this new identity'.[26] However, examining the Pike's history through the lens of scenography reveals the complexity of its aesthetic processes and political engagement. Reading historical source material concerning the Pike theatre from scenographic perspectives illuminates the company's inventive working processes, its modernizing strategies, its engagement with visual culture at a time when this was achieving an elevated cultural position, and its paradoxical championing and critique of internationalized modernity.

Space featured centrally in how co-founders Simpson and Carolyn Swift envisioned the Pike from the outset, as well as in their aspirations towards breaking new ground. Swift tells in her autobiography of how Simpson did not

---

[21] Pilkington, '*The Rose Tattoo* at the Dublin Theatre Festival', p. 24.

[22] Alan Simpson, *Beckett, Behan and a Theatre in Dublin* (London: Routledge and Kegan Paul, 1962), p. 1.

[23] Beckett was living in France and writing in French when the Pike requested the rights for the English language premiere of *Waiting for Godot*. While the English language premiere ended up taking place at the Arts Theatre Club, London in August 1955, the play enjoyed an extended run at the Pike, which subsequently toured Ireland, beginning in October that year. Behan's *The Quare Fellow* was initially rejected by the Abbey before being produced by the Pike in 1954.

[24] Pilkington, '*The Rose Tattoo* at the Dublin Theatre Festival', p. 27.

[25] Phyllis Ryan, *The Company I Kept* (Dublin: Townhouse, 1996), p. 140.

[26] Pilkington, '*The Rose Tattoo* at the Dublin Theatre Festival', p. 24.

want the Pike's home to be 'another little theatre' in the style of Studio or 37 Club; these, while staging new and challenging works, were located in Georgian basements, 'merely [offering] stages at the end of a large room'.[27] Swift and Simpson decided that a former coach house would be ideal; these buildings could be bought cheaply since they were generally used for storage, or as workshops or garages. After six months of searching, Swift and Simpson found the building that was to become the small Victorian-style Pike theatre on Herbert Lane.[28] The founders made the theatre a 'club', as this provided them a way to avoid 'complying with certain statutory regulations',[29] so technically a non-member could attend only as the guest of a paying member. Space also became an important factor in the company's artistic manifesto, which was printed in the first instalment of a regular newsletter that was sent out to its members:

> As our theatre is a small, intimate one, we intend to avail of the opportunities afforded to stage productions which, for various reasons, would not be seen on either the larger or smaller commercial stages, and we hope to give theatregoers opportunities to see more of the struggle going on at present in the world of theatre to introduce new techniques and new subjects in play writing. On the lighter side, we intend presenting late-night, intimate revue during Christmas and other holidays.[30]

Here, the spatial difference of the Pike is positioned as key to the intervention its founders sought to make in Irish theatre. In retrospect, Swift believes that the company carried out to the letter its opening manifesto. Drawing on Micheál Mac Liammóir, she adds that if 'the Abbey showed Ireland to herself, [...] [and] the Gate showed the world to Ireland' then the Pike 'wanted to show aspects of Ireland and the world which other theatres in Ireland were afraid or unable to show'.[31] Both spatially and in terms of its goals, the Pike sought to occupy a productive middle-ground.

The size of the stage space (twelve foot squared) had its limitations but this also inspired fruitful scenographic developments and effects.[32] According to Simpson, the smallness of the acting area prevented the Pike from presenting the first English language production of Ionesco's *The Chairs*; though a small portion of additional space could when necessary be borrowed from the scene dock, the stage was still not big enough to hold the amount of chairs necessary

---

[27] Carolyn Swift, *Stage by Stage* (Dublin: Poolbeg, 1985), p. 98.

[28] Swift, p. 99.

[29] Swift, p. 105.

[30] Swift, pp. 105-06.

[31] Swift, p. 106.

[32] Morash, in *A History of Irish Theatre*, has also refigured the limitations of the Pike theatre space as inciting creative possibilities, especially in lighting. He argues that Simpson's creative endeavours in this area emerged from the opportunities provided by both smallness and layout. Since 'no seat in the theatre was more than four rows back,' the audience never had a problem seeing the actors; this 'allowed Simpson to use almost exclusively directional toplights and sidelights, with very little spill, and only minimal front lighting was necessary to make the actors' faces visible' (p. 202).

to produce this work.[33] However, the Pike's small stage within its fifty-five seat auditorium also incited resourcefulness on Simpson's part in his regular role as lighting designer. Once the founders had their own premises, they were able to arrange for some of the floor of the room above the auditorium to be cut out in order to allow for a precisely-calculated throw of light.[34] Due to these renovations, Simpson claims that he was able to have much more lighting equipment than would have been possible in the larger theatres; through its use, he could curtail 'the difficulties caused by the close proximity of the audience to the stage and the smallness of the stage itself'.[35] He continues:

> I used a method of lighting which I learnt from watching ballet: this was to light from directly overhead and from the side, only using sufficient front lighting to heighten slightly the amount of light on the actors' faces. All the lighting I used was directional: that is to say, there was no spilling or flooding of light over the stage and, by this method, I achieved a three-dimensional emphasis on the actors which made the stage look bigger than it really was.[36]

This three-dimensional emphasis became a recurring feature throughout the Pike's repertoire. It is evident in several production photographs held in the Pike Theatre collections at Trinity College Library, Dublin, including images from *The Quare Fellow* (1954), *The Respectable Prostitute* (1956), *Posterity be Damned* (1959) and *The Solid Gold Cadillac* (1959).[37] These images showcase the chiaroscuro effect of Simpson's lighting, which sculpted definition on the actors' faces and bodies, and cast ominous shadows on the backdrop.

As Simpson reveals in his reference to ballet, the use of light to give the impression of amplified spatial dimensions, as well as to sculpt objects and actors' body-parts, was by no means new. The achievement of depth through the interplay of light and shadow actually characterizes some of the major innovations of twentieth-century scenography. Adolphe Appia, for example, began working on Richard Wagner's operas in the early twentieth century and is now considered a pioneer of modern scenography. He rejected flat scenic painting in favour of a more dynamic 'rhythmic space', created through the interactions of music, moving bodies, 'architectonic mass (steps, platforms, pillars, walls) and light'.[38] Appia harnessed lighting not just for its use value of enabling visibility but for its aesthetic function in also creating productive shadows and, as such, the depth that characterized his conception of rhythmic space. Simpson's lighting design, however, not only locates several of the Pike's productions within important twentieth-century developments in theatre scenography but within a zeitgeist in international visual culture at the time.

33 Simpson, p. 6.

34 Ibid., p.7.

35 Ibid., p. 6.

36 Ibid., pp.6-7.

37 Various images of these productions are held in the Pike Theatre Papers (General), Manuscripts and Archives Research Library, Trinity College, Dublin.

38 Joslin McKinney and Philip Butterworth, *The Cambridge Introduction to Scenography* (Cambridge: Cambridge University Press, 2009), p. 13.

Cinema was a popular recreational activity in 1950s' Ireland and film noir was a genre that Hollywood had popularized from the early 1940s on. One of its characteristic features – later to become clichéd – was its use of chiaroscuro lighting, a term appropriated from the work of Renaissance painters such as Caravaggio. Here, shadow was as important as light in constructing dramatic patterns of darkness and illumination to heighten suspenseful atmospheres.

While Simpson's approach to lighting appears to have been initially motivated by practicality rather than aesthetics (in that he sought at the outset to compromise for the smallness of the stage), for the Pike, the interplay of light, shadow and intimate space also helped to achieve sensual effects and make even more palpable intense dramatic moments, for example in its world premiere of Behan's *The Quare Fellow*. Although Simpson began by aiming through his lighting to make the stage area appear larger, many who attended this production commented on a sense of claustrophobia, which they attributed to the smallness of the theatre. Yet, according to Swift, this assumption 'does not give due credit to Alan's [Simpson's] production and lighting methods, deliberately designed to produce exactly that result'.[39] She exemplifies a moment in the play in which the prisoners speculate on what the Quare Fellow (the eponymous unseen convict who awaits execution) will be fed for his final meal. This scene was 'isolated in the Pike production by dimming the lights'.[40] The stark, simple set, consisting of five white door frames with plain black numbered doors constructed by Sean O'Shea, in conjunction with Simpson's lighting and the limited space both on stage and in the auditorium, must have added to the feeling – expressed by many of Behan's ex-prisoner friends who attended the production – of being back 'inside'.[41]

Christopher Baugh theorizes the interconnections of theatre technology and the advancement of scenography in the twentieth century, arguing that developments such as electric power underpin the scenographic approaches of Appia, Caspar Neher, Josef Svoboda and others.[42] The 'technologies' that the Pike used were far from advanced, but they showcased the theatre company's collective ingenuity. Although the Pike did have a few new spotlights, much of the lighting equipment consisted of old arena floods. The innovation lay in converting these into lanterns for the acting area through the addition of spill rings, while new floods were made using 'old biscuit tins' and 'operated from a second-hand dimmer board on which the dimmer was constantly jammed'.[43] The Pike was also inventive in its sound design. *The Quare Fellow* opened with a recording of Behan singing a rendition of 'The Ould Triangle', a prison song rumoured to have been written for the play by Behan's brother Dominic, who never actually claimed credit for it. The Pike hired a sound engineer who went, along with Behan and Rosamund Stevens (the theatre's publicity officer, who

---

[39] Swift, p. 143.
[40] Ibid.
[41] Simpson, p. 8.
[42] Christopher Baugh, *Theatre Performance and Technology: The Development of Scenography in the Twentieth Century* (Basingstoke: Palgrave Macmillan, 2005).
[43] Swift, p. 104.

also worked as a performer) to a large, empty hall to make the recording. Here, the natural echo of a prison, with its steel and concrete structures, could be replicated. Swift and Simpson both credit Stevens with this achievement, 'a very resourceful lady, capable of fulfilling the most difficult and improbable assignments'.[44] In this case, the improbable assignment included not only directing the recording, but ensuring that Behan had consumed just the right amount of liquor:

> Calculating carefully the amount of alcohol required to lubricate Brendan's tonsils without slurring his speech, she [Stevens] obtained a unique recording – on disc, for tape machines were still a thing of the future for Dublin theatres.[45]

The song itself, later made popular by the band The Dubliners, is already quite haunting. That quality must have been intensified by the distinctive sound of the Pike's recording filling its small and dimly lit auditorium as *The Quare Fellow* opened.

Scenographic Interactions

The scenography of the Pike theatre emerged through collaborative activities in which discrete professional roles and responsibilities became blurred. Simpson's army colleagues, who served with him in the Second Field Engineers from Clancy Barracks, made a vast contribution to the year-long renovation and refurbishment of the building, as well as the subsequent running of the theatre. Sergeant Edmund Kelly, for example, was the Pike's 'stage carpenter, electrician and resident stage manager all rolled into one' and so he was 'deservedly made a director of the theatre'.[46] Simpson, whose educational background was in engineering, had also worked with architects and building contractors in London.[47] Like many in the company, his role was that of a 'jack of all trades', working as director, set and/or lighting designer, and occasional writer and performer of deadpan comedy as part of the *Follies* – the name that the company gave to its late-night revue series. Swift worked as a performer, writer and director; painter Pauline Bewick began as a scenic designer but also became a star of the *Follies*; and Sheila Duncan doubled as costume-maker and choreographer. In *The Cambridge Introduction to Scenography* (2009), Joslin McKinney and Philip Butterworth position scenography as a collaborative process involving the interactions of any combination of individuals including but not limited to visual artists, designers, directors, lighting and sound specialists as well as performers, within a space and before an audience:

> The concept and practice of scenography does not promote existing hierarchies of roles and functions in the creation of theatre, dance or performance. Scenography and its production sit uneasily within the existing functions of writer, director, choreographer, designer and

[44] Simpson, p. 100.
[45] Swift, p. 144.
[46] Ibid., p. 102.
[47] Simpson, p. 3.

> performer because each, or any combination, of these roles is capable of producing scenography in ways that will not accept restriction implicitly imposed by such singular identities.[48]

From this perspective, scenography is a useful term because it is broader in its implications than 'theatre design', 'stage design' or 'mise en scène'.[49] Since it encompasses more of an inclusive, collaborative practice than singular, limited roles, it offers a way to reconsider the highly stratified value-structures of Irish theatre history. To acknowledge theatre scenography as a collective achievement is particularly useful when focusing on smaller theatre companies, as well as on a time and place in which very few professional stage designers were at work. In 1950s' Ireland, there were no educational institutions that provided professional training in stage design, and notably, the Abbey was without a resident designer from 1951 to 1964.

The Pike's *Follies*, in particular, were characterized by the spirit of collaboration. Swift led the *Follies* project, writing a significant portion of shows which invariably contained sketches devised by other members of the production team, as well as musical scores written or adapted by pianist George Desmond Hodnett. The *Follies* provided light entertainment and at times biting humour. Fittingly the scenic design made no attempt at realism, often featuring cloth backdrops painted in abstract or expressionistic designs by artists including Bewick and later Reginald Gray. Although it was arguably through these late-night revues that the Pike first established popularity and went on to ensure steady commercial stability, few scholarly works have discussed them in detail so far. Pilkington is a notable exception, offering some textual and scenographic analyses of the *Follies* in his book, *Theatre and the State* (2001),[50] and for context in his essay on the Pike's production of *The Rose Tattoo*.[51] There, he argues that:

> *The Rose Tattoo*, and the ideological effect of its performance, makes overt that which the satirical action of the popular 'follies' had only hinted at: that a somatic Irish modernity, so necessary and so reassuring to Ireland's new climate of modernization, could spill over into the erotic.[52]

Indeed, photographs held in the Pike Theatre collections evidence the ways in which women's costumes in particular became progressively skimpier from *The Follies of Herbert Lane* (1953) to *Pike Follies the Sun* (1959). Here, women's bodies exhibited a potential eroticism that threatened long-held nationalist conceptions of Ireland as sexually pure. Nevertheless, this was not the only way in which the *Follies* wrestled with the tensions of the period.

By 1957, the Pike 'had become the darling of Bord Fáilte, sponsors of the [Dublin Theatre] Festival, who kept ringing to request seats for distinguished

---

48 McKinney and Butterworth, p. 5.

49 Ibid.

50 Lionel Pilkington, *Theatre and the State in Twentieth-Century Ireland: Cultivating the People* (London: Routledge, 2001), p. 152.

51 Pilkington, 'The Rose Tattoo at the Dublin Theatre Festival', pp. 24-26.

52 Ibid., 'The Rose Tattoo at the Dublin Theatre Festival', p. 26.

foreign journalists'.[53] The Pike's programme of high modernist works from Europe and America, and support for new writing that helped to reimagine Ireland, certainly seemed to parallel the outward-looking, modernizing agenda of such government-sponsored initiatives as Bord Fáilte, An Tóstal and the Dublin Theatre Festival (which grew out of An Tóstal and aimed to foster intercultural tolerance). Trish McTighe aptly places the Pike's 1955 production of Beckett's *Waiting for Godot* 'in the context of a time when Ireland's tourism industry was at a very nascent stage, at the beginnings in Ireland of a determined and focused strategy of rural place and landscape marketing'.[54] McTighe focuses on the corresponding 'evocation of landscape' in the Pike's production of *Godot*.[55] Images of the West of Ireland became central to Bord Fáilte's branding. Indeed, Swift reveals that, with *Godot*, the Pike deliberately pointed to the West of Ireland through its set design:

> We used clothes, but painted in a mixture of browns and greens in blobs and sponges which, when lit, gave the effect of a continuous vista of what might be a bog, with a pathetic little willow in the foreground, its growth weakened and warped, as it would be in such a place, with nothing to shield it from the force of the west wind carrying rain clouds from the Atlantic.[56]

Judging by Swift's description, the Pike's scenographic interpretation of *Godot* appears both to initiate a process of reclaiming Beckett for Ireland that would culminate in the Gate's Beckett Festival in 1991,[57] and to reflect marketable, visual images of the rustic, romantic Irish West propagated by Bord Fáilte's rural place marketing.

The *Follies* responded differently to Ireland's expansionist engagement with the international. These revues mocked Blythe's preference for actors who could speak the Irish language at the Abbey. Meanwhile, many of the revues' acts seemed to revere foreignness. *Say it with Follies* (1956) featured Clare Dean, who was half-Indian, in two such numbers: 'Rum and Coca-Cola', a Cuban dance spot co-devised by Dean and Simpson in which Dean was adorned with plastic tropical fruit; and a performance of the Can-Can which accompanied Stevens singing 'But You Can in Cannes', a song by Swift that listed activities frowned upon or absent in various parts of Ireland that were possible in Cannes.[58] This awe for all things foreign bordered, at times, on

[53] Swift, p. 247.

[54] Trish McTighe, 'Landscapes and Literary Tourism: The Pike's *Godot* and the Commodification of Place in Ireland', paper delivered at 'The Irish and the City', Irish Society for Theatre Research conference at Birkbeck, University of London, 1 November 2013.

[55] Ibid.

[56] Swift, p. 190.

[57] For more on the Gate's role in reclaiming Beckett for Ireland, and for marketing the brand of an Irish Beckett internationally, see Trish McTighe, '"Getting Known": Beckett, Ireland and the Creative Industries', in Fintan Walsh, ed., *'That Was Us': Contemporary Irish Theatre and Performance* (London: Oberon 2013), pp. 160-62.

[58] Swift, pp. 227-29.

racial fetishism. 'The Lotus Flower Dance', for example, was presented as a serious number, choreographed by June Fryer and performed by Swift in *Further Follies* (1955). Here, Swift wore an elaborate costume based on Kathakali male attire complete with a papier-mâché headdress made by Desmond McNamara, to perform a dance derived from a mixture of Bharata Natyam steps. Swift herself admits that she was fortunate that her audience knew little enough about Indian dancing to figure out that the performance was, in fact, an inaccurate cultural mishmash.[59] Nevertheless, despite the sometimes unwitting caricaturing of other cultures, it appears that acts such as these aimed to further the Pike's support for internationalized modernity.

Yet the *Follies* also used satire to criticize the internationalization of Ireland and its move towards an export-driven economy. This was most evident in its engagement with scenographies outside the theatre. From the outset, the *Follies* showcased the interactions between scenography within and beyond the stage. For example, the first revue, *The Follies of Herbert Lane,* which premiered in December 1953, featured Michael Murray in mock ballet choreographed by Duncan dancing the role of the General Post Office's Statue of Cuchulainn. The most popular sketch that year was a satire on An Tóstal, which had been launched the previous April. Its subject was 'The Bowl of Light', erected by Dublin Corporation in an effort to decorate O'Connell Bridge in time for the festival. Intended to be a permanent structure, it consisted of a large octagonal basin containing multicoloured, plastic rotating flames. Some members of the public saw the structure as a monstrosity and, a few days after its unveiling, boisterous protests erupted. Weeks later, a student ended up breaking off the flames and throwing them in the river Liffey. The structure subsequently became known as 'the tomb of the unknown gurrier', and was eventually removed in 1963.[60] The Pike's first *Follies* presented Milo O'Shea as a personification of the Bowl of Light as it had been in all its glory. Playing the Ghost of the Tóstal flame, he wore a flaming headdress and surveyed Tóstals past and future, reciting:

> I'm the Ghost of the Tóstal Flame,
> And next Easter I'll add to my fame,
> With the Statue of Daniel O'Connell a dream,
> Done in chromium-plating – yes, that's the scheme.[61]

While the Pike would later be celebrated by Ireland's political establishment for subverting stale nationalist ideals, at this early stage the *Follies* can be seen also to participate in a public critique of nascent 'place marketing' endeavours which were being carried out scenographically through the decoration of Dublin city for An Tóstal.

---

[59] Ibid., p. 154.

[60] Keith Hopper, *Flann O'Brien: A Portrait of the Artist as a Young Post-modernist* (Cork: Cork University Press, 1995), pp. 270-75. Brian O'Nolan (Flann O'Brien) as Myles nagCopaleen is credited with first dubbing the bowel of light 'the tomb of the unknown gurrier'.

[61] Swift, p. 121.

A sketch called the Mannequin Parade also appeared in the *Follies* that year. This was a mock fashion show that poked fun at efforts to revamp the Irish fashion industry, which were taking place at the time with international competitiveness in mind. Here, the *Follies* can be seen both to reflect and to interrogate Ireland's push to develop its international exports. The sketch was to become an evolving part of future *Follies*. Although it parodied the Irish fashion industry, it became a regular feature of the *Fashion and Fun* shows in Ireland of the 1950s, where it was presented to audiences of over 1000 on large runways.[62] And while it mocked the processes of Ireland's internationalization, it also toured internationally as part of the *Dublin Pike Follies* which appeared at the Arts Theatre, Cambridge and the Lyric Theatre, Hammersmith in November 1957. A script for the sketch, with special additions and alterations for British audiences, is held in the Pike archive at Trinity College Dublin. The Mannequin Parade was narrated in 'honeyed tones' by Stevens, as fictional compere Neasa Ní Hemlchain.[63] The performers would model their outfits and silently mime various scenarios using their accessories and props in accordance with Ní Helmchain's presentation.

The Mannequin Parade derived its satire from the export-driven nation-branding that had become part of the Irish fashion industry. The *Dublin Pike Follies* version opens as follows:

> Ladies and Gentlemen, the Irish Fashion designers, Miss Sybil Connolly and Miss Irene Gilbert, have built up in Dublin a not inconsiderable export trade in haute couture – using and adapting Irish materials, such as tweed, to the haut couture of cities such as New York, Paris and Sydney. A really determined effort to boost Irish fashion exports to London, however, has not been thoroughly undertaken and it is with a view to capturing the fashion markets of London that we are presenting.

Specifically mentioning Connolly, who spearheaded efforts to revitalize the Irish fashion industry during the 1950s, the sketch also riffs on the drive to reintroduce traditional crafts such as tweed and embroidery as part of the Irish export trade.[64] The final male model is presented as a sort of plastic paddy figure. The outfit is entitled 'Gaelic Glory' and Ní Helmchain tells us that it is marketed towards the 'London-Irish nostalgic exiles'. The model carries a hurly, wears a 'bright blue suit, brown shoes, flashy American tie and a tweed cap', while Ní Helmchain tells us that 'the Irish patriot will note with satisfaction that not a single foreign influence has been at work in this model'. In addition to hinting at recent efforts to tempt the Irish diaspora through such

---

[62] Swift, p. 135.

[63] Swift, p. 120. In the manuscript, held in the Pike Theatre Papers (General), Trinity College, Dublin, 'Hemline' is written in brackets, presumably as the pronunciation for Nessa's surname 'Hemlchain' while on tour in the UK. All subsequent references to 'The Mannequin Parade' are from *Dublin Pike Follies* (November 1957), Pike Theatre Papers (General), Manuscripts and Archives Research Library, Trinity College, Dublin (MS 10813/6).

[64] Turpin, pp. 7-8.

initiatives as An Tóstal, the humour lies in the apparently inevitable transformation of the national by internationalism. Other offerings on the tour included Winsor Worthy, and the commuter conventional – an outfit positioned as perfect for men using London's public transport, complete with an umbrella which Ní Helmchain tells us is ideal for use in forcing one's way down an escalator. Here, as elsewhere in the *Follies*, the Pike plays with national stereotypes (in this case, both Irish and British) to produce comic effect. Yet, while The Mannequin Parade lampooned efforts to expand fashion and export industries, ironically it could also be seen in mutual co-optation with both. As well as showcasing the interactions of Ireland's theatrical and cultural scenographies, this exposes the intricate relationship that the Pike had with contemporary tensions concerning socio-economic change.

Conclusion

Ireland of the 1950s underwent what can be seen as a significant scenographic shift, in which visual culture was harnessed to improve Ireland's performance on the international stage. Examining the Pike theatre from the combined perspectives of established and emerging definitions of scenography reveals how Ireland's increasingly image-conscious culture impacted on the visual and performative character of Irish theatre. The Pike, by subverting traditional Irish nationalist ideals especially in its production of a work such as *The Rose Tattoo*, is usually remembered as part of efforts to achieve internationalized modernity following the Emergency, initially generated by Ireland's political establishment but apprehensively received by the public. Yet, the framework of scenography reveals much more about the complexity of the Pike's history in relation to contemporary visual and performative cultures. In its stage imagery, lighting and sound, the Pike can be seen to have contributed to the drive towards design innovation that characterized 1950s' Ireland. Simultaneously, however, the Pike can be seen as striving to negotiate the tensions of the period, especially through the scenography of the *Follies*. Throughout the life of the Pike, the *Follies* would continue to offer metatheatrical engagements with Irish visual culture and theatrical performance, for example by satirizing productions taking place on Ireland's larger commercial stages and by riffing on the Irish fashion industry even as a *Follies* sketch became part of its promotion. As such, the Pike can be seen to occupy a significant, self-conscious and complicated position in relation to Ireland's scenographic histories.

SIOBHÁN O'GORMAN is a postdoctoral researcher at the School of Drama, Film and Music, Trinity College Dublin. Her book project focuses on scenography in a modernizing Ireland, and is funded by the Irish Research Council. She taught at the English Department, NUI, Galway from 2008 to 2013, where she received a PhD for her thesis 'Negotiating Genders from the Page to the Stage.' Her work has appeared or is forthcoming in such publications as Irish Studies Review, Precarious Parenthood: Doing Family in Literature and Film, Verbal and Scene. She is co-editor of the forthcoming essay collection Devised Performance in Irish Theatre (Carysfort 2014) and was a critic for Irish Theatre Magazine from 2008 to 2014.

Fig. 1: Pat Duggan, Derry Power, Austin Byrne, Dermot Kelly, John McDarby and Pat Nolan in the premiere of *The Quare Fellow* (Act 1) at the Pike Theatre in 1954. Alan Simpson's lighting design often achieved a chiaroscuro effect. Here, this added to the sense of claustrophobia that characterized this production. Photograph by Andrew Flynn, courtesy of Manuscripts and Archives, Trinity College Library, Dublin.

Fig. 2: Carolyn Swift in the 'Lotus Flower Dance,' choreographed by June Fryer and performed as part of *Further Follies* (1955).

The *Follies* expressed awe for all things foreign, sometimes unwittingly caricaturing diverse cultures. Swift's costume was based on Kathakali male attire complete with a papier-mâché headdress made by Desmond McNamara, while the dance consisted of mixture of Bharata Natyam steps. Photograph by Andrew Flynn, courtesy of Manuscripts and Archives, Trinity College Library, Dublin.

Uneasy Bedfellows: Culture, Commerce and the Rise of the 'Production Hub' Paradigm in Irish Theatre

LISA FITZGERALD

[This article examines the rise and the resulting impact of the changing model for theatre funding in the years since the 2008 Irish banking crash. The production hub model of funding in Ireland has been introduced as an innovative and radical model of engagement, with burgeoning economic and cultural benefits for local communities. At the heart of this paradigm shift is the notion of how these funding structures 'perform'. The modification of traditional funding mechanisms has changed the landscape of theatre production in Ireland and the effects have yet to be ascertained. Through exploring the development of production hubs and project-based rather than company-based funding structures this article examines how these production hubs are performing. Interrogating the current rise in the production hub model and contextualizing within Irish and European policy trends, the aim of this article is to examine the implications of this shift in funding and deduce whether the theatre sector is better served by the sustained support of ongoing companies.]

Introduction

With the extent of Ireland's economic crisis materializing in 2008, the search for new funding models by local authorities, the Arts Council/An Chomhairle Ealaíon, and international support networks increasingly centred on the relationship between culture and commerce. Recent meetings by the Irish theatre research community such as the annual Irish Society for Theatre Research conference 'Perform or Else'[1] sought to examine new connections within theatre studies aligning the notion of performance with that of neo-

[1] 'Perform or Else' Annual Conference, Irish Society for Theatre Research (ISTR). NUI Galway, 26-28 October 2012.

liberalist capitalism.[2] The role of performance within a neo-liberalist framework associates human well-being with commercial entrepreneurship.[3] In Ireland new funding models emerged within this framework that engage directly with the relationship between economics and the arts. Terms rare within an Irish arts context – creative clustering, cultural assets, design economy, and creative capital – frequently recur in emerging Irish policy documents, for example, the 2008 'Building Ireland's Smart Economy' which sees the arts sector as a key economic contributor.[4] The reformation of the policy sector has resulted in the alignment of contemporary arts practice with cultural enterprise. One such policy framework, the production hub, is now a dominant force in theatre funding in Ireland.

The Arts Council experienced a reduction in funding from €84.6 million to €56 million between 2008 and 2014, resulting in the need for a theatre funding model that operates on a reduced budget. The production hub model of funding reflects a broader model of clustering which has emerged through wider EU and global initiatives. This article will interrogate the current rise in production hubs as both practice and policy, contextualized within Irish and European policy trends, and examine the implications of this shift in funding for current and future Irish theatre practice.

The Emergence of the Production Hub Phenomenon

The notion of hubs centred on creativity and innovation has emerged from the discourse between economics and creativity that forms part of the mechanics of neo-liberalism. A 2005 EU study, *The Economy of Culture in Europe*, defines hubs as 'creative networks within a geographical area. Their purpose is to develop a vision and strategy for growth for the creative sector with the local area, and then support the local sector in achieving it.'[5] Seen as an important element in the growth of the creative industry, hubs are founded on the idea of creative clustering as a dynamic way to foster creative growth. Creative clustering can be defined as the spatial grouping of cultural entities within a specific geographical area. Within this area, hubs essentially become a place where resources are pooled, partnerships emerge and there is an element of profit sharing in the dividends. URBACT, an EU programme promoting urban development describes creative clustering as emerging 'organically in specific urban frameworks through relations of production, work, research, education,

[2] Sessions included a roundtable discussion, 'Performance and Neo-Liberalism' with Rebecca Schneider, Lionel Pilkington and Helen Burke.

[3] David Harvey, 'Neoliberalism as Creative Destruction.' *Annals of the American Academy of Political and Social Science*, Vol. 610, NAFTA and Beyond: Alternative Perspectives in the Study of Global Trade and Development (Mar., 2007), pp. 22-44.

[4] Government of Ireland, *Building Ireland's Smart Economy; A Framework of Sustainable Economic Renewal* (Dublin: The Stationary Office. Dec 2008), p. 80. Available online http://www.taoiseach.gov.ie/attached_files/BuildingIrelandsSmartEconomy.pdf

[5] European Commission, The Economy of Culture in Europe, KEA European Affairs Chapter IV p. 169. Available online http://ec.europa.eu/culture/key-documents/doc873_en.htm

entertainment and leisure'[6] and cites the Digital Hub in Dublin as an example. More inclusive with a focus on organic growth from within the hub, the programme seems to herald an evolution towards more comprehensive policy-making. In Ireland, within theatre funding at least, this form of policy-making evolved from the idea of creative clustering to the production hub model. The previous success of creative clustering initiatives within regeneration projects across Ireland – such as the development of the Temple Bar area in Dublin – would bode well for a policy with a focus on shared resources and creative partnership.

Notwithstanding criticism of gentrification within regeneration projects, the policy of creative clustering has allowed for the successful creation of hubs in formerly deprived areas. Within this model cultural producers are economically viable and create work co-operatively, often using vacant spaces in post-boom cities. These clusters, an early example being the (now defunct) Temple Bar Cultural Trust's regeneration project in 1991,[7] have been initiated by groups and individuals in order to share resources, and have emerged both organically and increasingly as a form of state intervention. The concept of 'clustering' operates as a strategic response to diminished resourcing by both individuals and governments, concentrating cultural activity to achieve greater impact and reach in both artistic and economic terms. Projects such as the regeneration of Temple Bar in the south inner city of Dublin partly functioned to foster growth in declining urban areas, but also anticipated new models of cultural policy-making that today incorporate a broader range of cultural activities (particularly the creative industries) with very definite currency within the economy.

A creative hub that has emerged from the Temple Bar Regeneration project is the Project Arts Centre which the Arts Council recognizes as a 'de facto production hub'.[8] Yet despite the rapid embrace of clustering and the emergence of creative hubs as a means of driving regeneration projects in Ireland and across Europe, its outcomes and long-term impacts as state policy are far from clear. The widespread enthusiasm for the cluster phenomenon has not been tempered by moderate voices. As James Simmie observes, 'It has become the accepted wisdom more quickly than any other major idea in the field in recent years. This accelerated progress has been at the expense of

---

[6] URBACT II TN5. Creative Clusters in Low Density Urban Areas – Baseline Study. Creative clusters and the creative place: state of the art at EU level. (2008), p. 18. Available online http://urbact.eu/fileadmin/Projects/Creative_Clusters/State_of_the_art_EUlevel.pdf

[7] John McCarthy, 'Dublin's Temple Bar-A Case Study of Culture-led regeneration,' *European Planning Studies*, 6:3 (1998), pp. 271-81. John Montgomery, The Story of Temple Bar: Creating Dublin's Cultural Quarter', *Planning and Practice*, 10:2, pp. 135-72.

[8] Arts Council/An Chomhairle Ealaíon, *Supporting the Production and Presentation of Theatre-A New Approach*, (Dublin: Arts Council/An Chomhairle Ealaíon, March 2010), p. 6.

previous explanations and lacking in relevant empirical evidence'.[9] The creative cluster approach – with its origins in localized, radicalized cultural entrepreneurial hubs – has now extended beyond its original association with urban regeneration to influence new forms of funding and lacks as Simmie notes a broad examination of the impact on cultural producers.

In contemporary Irish theatre practice, the recent policy shift away from the sustained support of ongoing theatre companies towards an emphasis on hubs as centres for cultural production has created unease amongst theatre practitioners. The already precarious nature of theatre work has been exacerbated by the instability and lack of transparency surrounding the production hub model. Rather than reinforcing the support structures in place for theatre workers, there has been a growing anxiety within the sector that scarcity of support is being repackaged as a dynamic model of funding.

Irish Historical Background to the Production Hub Model

In 2005, a policy paper entitled *Theatre-Background Discussion Paper* was published by the Arts Council. It outlines the need for an increased structural and critical framework for theatre practitioners in Ireland, without which, theatre will essentially remain haphazard 'impaired by its lack of knowledge of performance theory, the absence of adequate and flexible performance spaces, poor current marketing information, and the deprivation of the safe critical space provided by formative training methodology in all areas of practice'.[10] Creating a new framework for Arts funding, the policy document *Partnership for the Arts: In Practice 2006-2008*, published in December 2005, listed five goals: to affirm and promote the value of theatre in society, to assist theatre artists in realizing their artistic ambitions, to make it possible for people to extend and enhance their experiences of theatre, to strengthen arts organizations countrywide, and to ensure the Arts Council works effectively to support theatre.[11] The document emphasizes the need for increased partnership and collaboration across disciplinary boundaries: 'The initiatives, advocacy and funding programmes relate equally to multi-disciplinary organisations with an interest in, or a role to play, within that artform.'[12] This move towards organizations and artists that work across disciplines marks an important shift from the support of the traditional theatre company model, with its emphasis on a core ensemble. A position paper on the traditional model of theatre funding published by the Arts Council in 2005 describes the issues that make it increasingly infeasible. It criticizes the traditional model of funding with

---

[9] James Simmie, (2006). 'Do Clusters or Innovation Systems Drive Competitiveness?' in Bjørn Asheim, Philip Cooke and Ron Martin, eds., *Clusters and Regional Development: Critical Reflections and Explorations* (Oxon: Routledge, 2006), p. 184.

[10] Arts Council/An Chomhairle Ealaíon, *Theatre-Background Discussion Paper*, (Dublin: Arts Council/An Chomhairle Ealaíon, 2005), p. 4.

[11] Arts Council/An Chomhairle Ealaíon, *Partnership for the Arts: in Practice 2006-2008*, (Dublin: Arts Council/An Chomhairle Ealaíon, 2005), p. 32.

[12] Ibid., p. 4.

theatrical organizations divided into a fixed component namely a board of directors, an artistic director, a company manager and a more fluid component, those hired on contract per production. The main criticism was the unnecessary costs of the fixed component which 'often drain resources unduly, thereby limiting companies' ambition and their capacity to create a viable body of work'.[13]

Following the financial crisis and subsequent guarantee of the banking system by the Fianna Fáil government in September 2008, the funding to the theatre sector was slashed. A discussion document published in May 2009, *Examining New Ways to Fund the Production and Presentation of Theatre*, acknowledges previous concerns about the non-viability of the traditional theatre company model: 'While the current economic crises and the reduction in the Art Council's own resources have exacerbated the challenges, they have not of themselves been the cause of this dilemma.'[14] The document outlines the problems with the theatre company-funding model noting that is 'not sustainable, given finite resources'.[15] It criticizes traditional patterns of funding that place 'too much emphasis on the Production Company as a model'.[16] In offering alternatives and inviting responses from theatre practitioners, the document lists a new model of support where the Arts Council will provide once-off funding to practitioners working outside of the traditional theatre company funding model. This model would extend and offer additional measures to the practice of once off funding already in existence. These additional measures might include the funding of administrative service providers that would facilitate the work of the artists. The document notes that: 'While this concept of an administrative support has been referred to as "Production Hubs", the specific detail of how such administrative support might operate in practice has not yet been defined.'[17] This new model of funding would provide a more flexible way of funding theatre practitioners without the fixed components of the traditional model i.e. the board of directors, company manager, artistic director that was considered a financial drain on important resources. Importantly this document points to not only the introduction of the 'production hub model' specifically but also the lack of clarity around how this model might operate in practice.

Generating enthusiasm for this new form of funding, the language used in government documents focuses on the opportunities that would emerge for theatre makers. This new model suggests that it will allow theatre to become part of the community rather than being enclosed in the conventional theatre space. Moving out from traditional theatrical structures, practitioners cluster around specific projects rather than relying on annual funding. This new format

[13] Qtd. in Arts Council/An Chomhairle Ealaíon, *Examining New Ways to Fund the Production and Presentation of Theatre: Discussion Document*. (Dublin: Arts Council/An Chomhairle Ealaíon, 2009), p. 4.

[14] Ibid., p. 5.

[15] Ibid., p. 6.

[16] Ibid., p. 6.

[17] Ibid., p. 7.

would allow for a vibrant and progressive interplay between theatrical performance and the community. This rhetoric did tap into a deep-rooted resentment of traditional models of funding which channelled money into duplicated administration costs across a multitude of theatre companies. The need to review production models, articulated here as a means of deepening community engagement, also clearly bore an economic dimension as David Parnell, Head of Theatre at the Arts Council commented, the current financial crisis 'is a good opportunity to at least re-imagine the model by which we make theatre'.[18]

Since 2009 the traditional theatre funding model in Ireland with annual funding to production companies has been scaled down in favour of alternative modes of support. In the Arts Council paper, *Supporting the Production and Presentation of Theatre-A New Approach*, the delineation was made between the traditional theatre model and the newly embraced production hub model stating that 'while we recognise that some artists might choose the production company model as the ideal vehicle through which to realise their artistic ambitions, the level of resources available to the Arts Council only permits a limited number of production companies to be fully supported'.[19] As part of their new funding strategy articulated by this document, the Arts Council outlined six complementary types of support; the third being 'shared administrative resources' where the term production hub was defined as a method of sharing resources. The model facilitated the production and presentation of the work of more than one artist or 'production entity' and 'can play a valid role as part of a balanced theatre ecology by virtue of the fact that it is more cost effective to provide funding for administrative resources that are shared'.[20]

Past and Present: Production Hubs in Practice

The *Supporting the Production and Presentation of Theatre—A New Approach* (2010) document highlights the use of the production hub paradigm as a cost-effective measure with the pooling of resources an answer to the financial straightening brought on by budget cuts. The notion of the production hub, however, is not an entirely new concept in terms of Irish arts funding. Peter Crawley made the point in a 2009 article that 'The Project Arts Centre in Dublin ... has long functioned as a *de facto* hub by extending its administrative and technical resources to a number of associated artists who are then freed up to make work without the daily concerns and running costs of maintaining a company.'[21] In *Supporting the Production and Presentation of Theatre*, the Arts Council, as stated earlier, recognizes that there was already a number of

[18] Peter Crawley, 'Fall of the Small after Unkindest Cuts of all,' *Irish Times*, 2 February 2009. p. 16.

[19] Arts Council/An Chomhairle Ealaíon, *Supporting the Production and Presentation of Theatre-A New Approach*, (Dublin: Arts Council/An Chomhairle Ealaíon, March 2010,) p. 4

[20] Ibid., p. 5.

[21] Peter Crawley, 'Getting to the hub of the issue,' *Irish Times*, 4 June 2009.

what they termed 'de facto production hubs' operating.[22] Along with the Project Arts Centre, the Dublin Fringe Festival and Cork Midsummer Festival were offered as examples where 'the evidence to date supports the view that they are efficient, on the basis that they can facilitate a number of artists (or producing entities) to create their work at the same time, without each individual feeling it is necessary to set up a company limited by guarantee.'[23] These established hubs could prove invaluable, as they are already confronting the issues that future production hubs will face. The difference between these older production hub models and the newer hubs is thus: the newer model represents an economy measure for the Arts Council at a time of reduced funding rather than a bona fide endorsement of a different method of funding.

In response to the Arts Council paper, Loughlin Deegan, Director of The Lir, questions 'whether we can have a healthy theatre infrastructure using this model. I think we need further discussion, more information and further insights into the Council's thinking and their plans for the future.'[24] The lack of a definitive framework of knowledge and expertise is evident in confusion surrounding the transparency of the hub model. The fact that there are existing examples of the hub model that have evolved separate to the emerging governmental policy should provide a framework of reference with respect to the implementation of shared administration costs and other overheads.

The first to use the production hub model as designated by the Arts Council is the Limerick theatre hub in 2009. Based in the Belltable Arts Centre (which has since closed down in January 2013) the 'Elements' season created four productions using shared resources and personnel. Each production corresponded to a particular element; Air: *Excess Baggage* by Mary Coll, Water: *The Fisherman's Son* by Ciarda Tobin, Fire: *Don Juan in Hell* by George Bernard Shaw, and Earth: *The Revenger's Tragedy* by Mike Finn. They were staged at the Belltable's blackbox interim space between 15 June and 21 November 2010. Funding was awarded through the Arts Council's 'Projects: Once Off Awards' and came to €86,000. In his 2010 evaluation report of the project, Dr Michael Finneran noted that 'open communication with the Arts Council through the offices of David Parnell, Head of Theatre & Circus and Val Ballance, Head of Venues, was maintained throughout the conceptualisation and formulation of the *LTH* proposal'.[25] Crucially in this open communication with the Arts Council, Finneran points out that 'strong expressions of support for the possibilities inherent in a theatre hub model were received.'[26]

Then Artistic Director of the Belltable Arts Centre Joanne Beirne felt that 'the Hub should be a professional programme of work for an audience, yes, but also that it would facilitate artists getting to the level of producing work of a

---

[22] Arts Council/An Chomhairle Ealaíon, Supporting the Production and Presentation of Theatre-A New Approach, (March, 2010), p. 6.

[23] Ibid., p. 6.

[24] Peter Crawley, 'A New Policy for Theatre: Theatre Forum Responds,' *Irish Theatre Magazine,* 12 May 2010.

[25] Michael Finneran, The Limerick Theatre Hub 2009 Evaluation Report, (2010), p. 8.

[26] Ibid.

professional quality themselves in the future'.[27] The changing landscape in the structuring of theatre production was evidenced in this new model for funding that the Arts Council were clearly moving towards at the time. Concluding his report, Finneran made the point that the context within which the hub was awarded funding is important. The fact that Ireland was in the throes of a financial crisis meant that alternative and more cost-effective methods of theatre production were needed: 'one could argue that it was indeed prudent that the Arts Council began to explore alternative models of funding theatre work, particularly in regional cities.'[28] The funding model introduced at the Limerick Theatre Hub was concerned more with commercial and financial restraints in the face of increasing cutbacks as opposed to artistic concerns. Although the production hub model has benefits (in that it creates a space for increased collaboration between theatre practitioners) the short-lived and precarious nature of the framework – as seen in the case of the Limerick Theatre Hub – has generated some anxiety among the theatre community.

In rolling out production hubs as alternative models of funding, the Arts Council has slashed financial support to established theatre companies. On 1 February 2010 they announced that funding to theatre practice was cut from €16,311,000 to €13,327,000. Eleven companies had their funds discontinued entirely, amongst them Barabbas and Meridian, long-established and successful theatre companies. That same year other companies had their funding severely cut, including 48% for the Corn Exchange and 35% for the Performance Corporation. The Arts Council budget stood at €65.16 million in 2011. In 2012 the total Arts Council budget was €63.2 million, of which the annual theatre funding stood at €11,582,416, distributed amongst 134 arts organizations. The Arts Council budget was cut to €59.9 million in 2013 and the current 2014 funding for the Arts Council stands at €56 million.

The continuous cutbacks to the arts sector have led to resentment amongst theatre practitioners with responses such as Jo Mangan of the Performance Corporation illustrating the effect funding cuts were having on the sector: 'Many of my colleagues have had their life's work and their livelihoods annihilated overnight without being offered any realistic way of continuing to create work for Irish audiences.'[29] The introduction of the production hub model of funding in light of the low morale instigated by detrimental funding cuts led to suspicion that the model was an opportunity for more stealth cuts in the theatre sector. A significant difficulty with the production hub model is the negative impact on supporting career paths of theatre practitioners, since funding is received on an *ad hoc* project-by-project basis. Former Theatre Forum Chairperson Fergal McGrath has voiced such concerns: 'It is clear... that the role of the company model is effectively being reduced. Most feedback we've been getting is that it raises the question, what becomes of the shelf life of

[27] Sara Keating, 'At the Hub of Limerick's Theatre Life,' *Irish Theatre Magazine*, 8 December 2009.
[28] Michael Finneran, p. 14.
[29] Sue Conley, 'Our Work Cut Out,' *The Herald*, 11 February 2010.

productions, employment of artists, and do career paths exist anymore?'[30] Whether the production hub can hold or echo the successes brought by the theatre company model is not established, but what is certain is that it will produce work for less funding.

The issue was exacerbated by the fear that the production hub model was to replace the traditional – and previously very successful – theatre company model. Former director of the Belltable Arts Centre, Joanne Beirne, makes the point that the traditional theatre company model is more suited to establishing what she terms 'a continuity of vision'.[31] The haphazard nature of the 'hub' model of funding does not support an ongoing exploration of thematic concerns for one theatre producing entity. Some theatre groups have expressed frustration concerning the lack of clarity about the implementation of production hubs, and how the proposed clustering will work as part of an integrated policy incorporating existing arts structures. Jane Daly of the Irish Theatre Institute has noted that there is 'a need to establish some sense of stability rather than deconstruct the existing infrastructure, which is already fragile'.[32] The focus within the production hub model on *ad hoc* funding proved worrying for theatre practitioners who also felt that such a model would also create an environment of prescriptive funding. Director and Founder of Dance Theatre of Ireland, Loretta Yurick, has pointed out that the Arts Council has 'decided who should make what work and where. It's prescriptive funding... We're incapacitated'.[33] The onus would be on the maker of the work to continually be at the remit of the funder. This type of funding would stifle the creativity that had been at the heart of the traditional theatre company model.

Strengths and Weaknesses: Fallout for Theatre Practice in Ireland

It is beneficial to see the production hub model not just within an Irish framework but as part of a broader move towards hub or cluster funding. The move towards an increased commercialization of the arts is in part due to the financial constraints of the recent economic crisis but is also part of a wider trend toward the clustering of multidisciplinary organizations in the creative sector. As discussed in the Introduction, the shift towards the 'economization' of the arts and the positioning of the arts within a 'creative economy' has become an integral part of policy-making at a trans-national level. The 'creative cluster' paradigm which has its origins in the hubs that blossomed in urban regeneration programmes is an appropriate approach for the production hub model in an Irish context.

In its policy document outlining the strategy for developing the arts in Ireland until 2013, the Arts Council cites 'creative and cultural industries' as

---

30 Peter Crawley, 'A New Policy for Theatre: Theatre Forum Responds,' *Irish Theatre Magazine*, 12 May 2010.

31 Peter Crawley, 'Getting to the hub of the issue.'

32 Justine Nakase and Roisín Stack. 'Keeping a Head Above Water: Irish Theatre in a time of Transition,' *New Hibernia Review*, 13: 3 (2009), p. 125.

33 Rosita Boland, 'Death by a thousand Cuts,' *Irish Times*, 17 September 2010.

one of its key areas of partnership and highlights the need 'to explore the establishment of a partnership framework to develop these links'.[34] This type of language and its introduction to the arts sector has been part of a European model of funding that is now becoming increasingly evident in Ireland. The use of creative industries to drive economic growth supports a mode of funding that is considered more entrepreneurial – the production hub model – than passive like the theatre company model. Chris Bilton looks at how cultural policy can move from a static and passive model dependent on state funding towards what he terms a 'systems view' of creativity which leads to 'an appreciation of the infrastructure, networks and collaborations which underpin the visible peaks of creative output'.[35] This view of creativity which focuses on infrastructure, networks and collaboration rather than the visible peaks of creative output could also be attached to the production hub model of theatre production. The creation and support of hubs rather than the insular and tight-knit groupings of the theatre company model could prove to be more dynamic in the creation of experimental and innovative theatre.

The rise in the production hub model has certainly proved divisive amongst the theatre community. The economic and cultural benefits are pitted against a suspicion that the model is an attempt to deliver cutbacks masquerading as a new and innovative form of funding. Cultural enterprise is a marrying of cultural policy and artistic enterprise, and ultimately is dependent on the success of artistic endeavours. The enthusiasm for the production hub model of funding is understandable, given its potential for quick and radical results. However, with that enthusiasm there is a potential for a lack of analysis and exploration of the long-term effects this change in funding would have on established policy practice.

Although many theatre practitioners have voiced concern over the production hub model, there has also been positive outlook for potential in the future. Reporting on the Limerick Theatre Hub, discussed earlier in the article, Sara Keating described an 'impressive creative enterprise' which resulted in productions where there was 'a recognizable consistency to the production values of the four plays'. Despite low audience attendance (attributed to the material covered by the plays), Keating notes that the hub had 'successfully demonstrated that there is a huge talent among the theatre community in the region, and it has also proved the hub model is capable of producing consistent and excellent work'.[36] In an article on the Limerick Theatre Hub Peter Crawley commented that 'if the Belltable demonstrates that more productions can be generated with a comparatively lower level of investment into a central hub, the company model that has characterised Irish theatre for a generation may

[34] Arts Council/An Chomhairle Ealaíon, *Developing the Arts in Ireland: Arts Council Strategic Overview 2011-2013*, (Dublin: Arts Council/An Chomhairle Ealaíon, 2010) p. 14.

[35] Chris Bilton, *Management and Creativity: From Creative Industries to Creative Management*, (Oxford: Blackwell, 2007) pp. 166-67.

[36] Sara Keating, 'At the Hub of Limerick's Theatre Life.'

appear redundant.'[37] Such remarks suggest that production hubs can create good theatre under difficult conditions and in the right circumstances can benefit from the new relationships that arise in the atmosphere of co-operation. However, the unfortunate closing of the Belltable in March 2013 indicates that – given the current economic climate – even with shared resources the arts infrastructure is predisposed to collapse.

It is understandable that there has been reluctance on the part of theatre practitioners to relinquish the older model of theatre companies operating a consistent output of performances and nurturing young and emerging talent, be it in stage management, playwriting, directing, and so on. As a measure of success, traditional funding models have resulted in the creation of innovate, ground-breaking theatre through the support of companies such as Galway's Druid Theatre Company and their pioneering work with playwrights such as Martin McDonagh and Enda Walsh. Cork's Corcadorca has also emerged as a trailblazer in site-specific performance in Ireland. Although these companies will still receive core company seed funding, it is the emerging theatre companies that may not benefit from this annual stable funding irrespective of output or performance reception. The role that theatre companies have to play within production hubs and their interest in doing so is yet to be ascertained. In his recommendations about the Limerick Theatre Hub, Finneran suggests that 'existing theatre companies who participate in hubs should be recognised as entities in their own right, but must also be a part of the hubs and share in the common objectives and decision-making processes of the hub for the duration of the funding'.[38]

Ultimately national and regional theatre can be challenged and revitalized by engaging with new modes of interaction and models of creation initiated through different types of funding. However, the production hub model is a direct result of cultural policy rather than a grass-roots movement. Creative clustering in the form of production hubs will transform the theatrical process in Ireland, but crucial to its success is a continuing negotiation between the people making the theatre and the structures supporting them. Economic imperatives and the resulting new models of theatre funding need to lay a sustainable foundation which supports new and dynamic modes of theatre production while still encompassing traditional structures. Fears have emerged (such as those voiced by Loretta Yurick) that the sporadic and somewhat nomadic work of the production hubs model and the clustering of theatre practitioners in varying projects will destabilize a successful framework for theatre-making.

However, although the production hub model is recognized as a more haphazard approach than the traditional safety net of annual funding, the model has and will encourage more collaboration. Shared resources will also free theatre practitioners to focus on creative work rather than administrative obligations. Within larger umbrella hubs such as the 2014 Limerick City of

---

[37] Peter Crawley, 'Getting to the hub of the issue.' p. 18.
[38] Michael Finneran, p. 24.

Culture or the Decade of Centenaries programme the opportunity is there for individual and group theatre practitioners to engage in collaborative work. The Professional Limerick Artists Network which emerged in response to the 2013 closure of the Belltable Arts Centre in Limerick issued *An Assessment of the Current Needs of Artists Working in Limerick*. The assessment made the point that theatre practitioners have been gathering together through the PLAN and Limerick City of Culture meetings and the theatre community 'collectively, is now discussing collaboration and sharing of ideas with a view to creating a landmark theatre event as part of the city's designation [city of culture]'.[39]

The fallout from the Limerick City of Culture fiasco saw the resignation of artistic director Karl Wallace and two advisors, Jo Mangan and Maeve McGrath, due to differences with the board over programming choices. What became evident from these tensions is the pitfalls of working in collaboration with groups that may not share agreed artistic concerns. The cost of staging the work of renowned French street theatre company, Royal de Luxe, as part of the Limerick City of Culture proved fractious for the organizers. Budgetary concerns surfaced due to the expense of the French theatre company and the board could not reach consensus causing subsequent resignations. Karl Wallace highlights the opportunity to learn from the Limerick City of Culture debacle: 'it's essential that a collaborative relationship is established with the local authority, and indeed this might result in good future working practices. However, this takes time, planning and research.'[40] Guidelines for good practice in the collaborative efforts between groups with sometimes disparate interests are crucial to the functioning of hubs. These guidelines are not yet established and the *ad hoc* nature of the hubs maintains an unstable rather than a dynamic framework for creating work.

Conclusion

This article sought to examine the current rise in production hubs as both practice and policy, contextualized within Irish and European policy trends, and examine the implications of this shift in funding for current and future Irish theatre practice. The emergence of culture as an economy has resulted in its practitioners being seen as workers selling a commercially valuable commodity; culture. This in itself is not necessarily a wholly negative result. The culture industry within the EU and global discourse comes from a dynamic and positivist discourse eager to channel more inclusive process-orientated modes of funding. The problem is that in an Irish context the policies do not stem from this discourse but represent an economic measure at a time of reduced funding. Sharing administration costs and pooling resources does create a more flexible model of theatre production. It frees up theatre makers to

[39] Professional Limerick Artists Network. An Arts Assessment of the Current Needs of Artists working in Limerick, May 24th 2013, p. 8.

[40] Laurence Mackin, 'Karl Wallace: A very Delicate Balance,' *Irish Times*, 11 January 2014.

focus on production rather than administration, but it is wrong to suggest that it is a new mode of funding and it has the potential to make invisible the conditions through which work is being produced.

Although the impetus for change is evident amongst theatre practitioners, as is their willingness to cooperate in the creation of production hubs, there remains a clear need for a national evaluation of the changing practice of theatre funding. The lack of coherence is not serving the theatre community and the next step in the support of theatre practice is to create a framework of knowledge and expertise that will integrate the production hub model further. This evaluation could – through in-depth discussion with the theatre community and evaluation of the theatre landscape – make recommendations that will facilitate a more integrated, dynamic and transparent model for funding theatre in Ireland. The unfortunate fallout from the change in the funding landscape since 2008 is the fear that there is a fixed binary framework for the production of theatre – the either/or model does not work in theory, and it does not work in practice. The relationship between theatre and commerce is increasingly inter-dependent. The fear is that in the increasing commodification of the Irish cultural landscape, cultural heritage, – of which the theatre is so much a part – will be squandered.

LISA FITZGERALD is a PhD candidate in Theatre and Performance Studies based in the National University of Ireland, Galway. Her research interests include ecocriticism, site-specific performance, cultural heritage and the archive. Previous research projects have explored the relationship between site-specific theatre performance and historic sites throughout Ireland. Currently she is concerned with reassessing the work of Irish theatre through an ecocritical lens and examining the intersection between geographical/-landscape studies and theatre performance.

Respond or Else: Conor McPherson's *The Weir* at the Donmar Warehouse

EAMONN JORDAN

This article is an interrogation of both the production of Conor McPherson's *The Weir* at the Donmar Warehouse (2013) and of my own positioning as a critic and commentator of this performance. Taking my lead from W.B. Worthen's question 'What are dramatic performances performances of?', I pose the alternative question what is a performance analysis an analysis of? (To that end, I want to contest the shorthand use of the notion of 'the audience' or 'the spectator' as an expression of some unifying and global point of view.)

The article notes how far the experience is from being a passively observed experience, shaped fundamentally by my seated presence and proximity to the stage. Instead, my embodied act of spectatorship is a far more fundamental act of involved consciousness inspired by the pace, the energies and sensations, rhythms, movements, perspectives and shifts in register emanating from Josie Rourke's mise-en-scène that are then absorbed, mirrored back and creatively and imaginatively inflected by my own knowledge, experiences, attitudes, commitment, participation and presence. These are seen in light of a whole variety of questions, biases, anticipations, expectations and tangential considerations that are novel and personal.]

For anyone sitting in the auditorium of the Donmar Warehouse in London on 2 May 2013 for the first major London revival of Conor McPherson's *The Weir*, by Josie Rourke, since its premiere at the Royal Court in 1997,[1] there are lots of prior questions, heightened expectations, feelings of enthusiasm and also some

[1] In 1998 at The Gate Theatre in Dublin I saw the Royal Court touring production, directed by Ian Rickson, which had won Olivier, Evening Standard and Critics' Circle Awards in 1997. In 2008, I saw a production at the Gate, directed by Garry Hynes.

anxieties.[2] I also have in mind an awareness of W.B. Worthen's question, 'What are dramatic performances performances *of*?'[3] Worthen's response is to say that 'The text is absorbed into the multifarious verbal and non-verbal discourses of theatrical production, transformed into an entirely incommensurable thing, an event.'[4] So in that absorption and transformation, Worthen wonders, 'How can dramatic performance be conceived not as the performance of the text but as an act of iteration, an utterance, a surrogate standing in that positions, uses, signifies the text within the citational practices of performance'?[5]

In terms of critical response here is a parallel question that builds on from Worthen's: 'What is a performance analysis an analysis *of*? This paper will illustrate the variables that shape my responses. By this performance at the Donmar Warehouse I presumed I would be reminded of certain issues central to the text and to be engaged by what I may have ignored or missed out on in my previous distillations of this play's dramaturgy and in my processing of prior performance experiences. More broadly, I also hoped to upgrade and re-invigorate my own thinking about this play, as I accept that I am a somewhat different person to the one who published first about it in 2004.[6] I also wished to investigate if there were things that Rourke's production did not unduly emphasize, but were issues I had previously prioritized and maybe even had over-estimated their significances in my own reflections and contextualisations. Additionally, might there be issues that are potentially repressed within the current *mise-en-scène*? I also wanted to consider how the performance processed some of the theoretical propositions that I had in mind in relation to masculinity, femininity, and the significances of narrative and pastoral spaces in terms of this work. I also wished to think through some of the more recent academic commentary which positioned *The Weir* far more in relation to

---

[2] See Helen Warner's production photographs http://www.helenwarner.co.uk/the-weir-at-the-donmar-warehouse-production-photographs-2/.

[3] W.B. Worthen, 'Drama, Performativity, and Performance', *PMLA*, 113.5 (Oct 1998), pp. 1093-107, 1101.

[4] Ibid., p.1101.

[5] Ibid., p.1102.

[6] There is also a certain anxiety about repeating my own previous responses to this work, consequently I plan not to peruse what I have written about this play until I am close to having a final draft, and will read a different edition of the play-text in order to avoid latching on to the lines and stage directions that I had previously marked, and responding to the comments that I have made in the margins. I will also anticipate some of the criticism I plan to read and respond to before I complete this piece and will only scan reviews at a late stage to see if there is any detail of importance that I missed. See Eamonn Jordan, 'Pastoral Exhibits: Narrating Authenticities in Conor McPherson's *The Weir*', *Irish University Review*, 34:2 (Autumn-Winter 2004), pp. 351-68. (Noted is my own glaring error in calling those Danish or Norwegian tourists, inaccurately labelled 'Germans' by the play's characters, as 'non-nationals' (p. 357), rather than as non-Irish nationals.) I also co-edited with Lilian Chambers, *The Theatre of Conor McPherson: Right Beside the Beyond* (Dublin: Carysfort Press, 2012).

Ireland's Celtic Tiger economic boom than I myself had previously acknowledged.[7]

As a consequence I am conscious that I want my responses to Rourke's production not to be a comparison with other productions that I had seen, and by calling attention to various interdigiting factors, I would like it to be more than simply a response to a performance. This is more about the interface between critical frameworks and my own scholarship, a range of research ideas and my own experiences, expectations, and positive attitude to McPherson's body of work more generally. I am alert to the fact that I would intuitively resist negative readings of masculinity in his work and of either the monologue form or his quasi-naturalist instincts, however much he accommodates the supernatural in such stage environments. Even amongst the best of recent scholarship on Irish theatre, much of it is overly dependent on or utterly blind-sighted by an obsessive impulse towards theoretical framing, to such an extent that text and performance seem to be merely incidental or irrelevant aspects. I want also to shy away from that sort of critical positioning, believing firmly in the need to ground arguments in precise detail and clear cut, unspeculative evidence.

During the performance, I only record in my notebook essential details, trusting the rest to my memory. I will also study the stage design in detail before and after the performance. Finally, I want to respond to the substances and absences of this performance in ways that are hopefully nuanced, open and insightful, whilst ultimately accepting that many of these responses are inflected and determined by my own prior associations with and attitudes towards the play. The challenge in many ways is summed up by Bruce McConachie's term 'cognitive multitasking'.[8] And my performance analysis will be a form of critical 'unmasking', recognizing that an act of criticism is not simply a response, but is overlain with many diverse inputs, competencies, expectations and knowledge, as already suggested.

Through the Bottom of a Glass

Fictionalized rural Irish spaces are often associated with beauty, isolation, history, with pre-lapsarian fantasies, with the exploitative practices of landlords, with pagan or Christian religion, with hardship, exile and a nostalgia for things long past. Tom Scutt's elaborate and highly detailed design goes a long way towards setting and maintaining the atmosphere and mood of the

---

[7] Additionally, in October 2012 I had seen a Druid Theatre Company production of Tom Murphy's *Conversations on a Homecoming* (1983), directed by Garry Hynes, and I was reminded of its huge influence on *The Weir*. (Both plays have an extensive evening's drinking compressed into less than a two hour performance time.) The previous productions of *The Weir* that I had seen, including one directed by Hynes, had little of the anger that drives this work by Murphy. But I wondered if *The Weir* could entice an aggrieved or angrier sort of production, particularly in light of an awareness of the economic collapse suffered by Irish citizens from late 2007.

[8] Bruce McConachie, *Engaging Audiences: A Cognitive Approach to Spectating in the Theatre* (Basingstoke: Palgrave, 2008), p. 28.

piece. In the very intimate 300 seat Donmar Warehouse space, the bar/pub environment fills the whole performance environment. In Scutt's design there are exposed wooden beams overhead and the floor is tiled rather than carpeted. (This is a particularly important detail according to the stage designer, who notes how the floor is tiled so 'that the guys in the pub sense that the sound of Dervla [Kirwan as Valerie] is very different to the shuffle' of Brian Cox's Jack.)[9] Also, there is a somewhat visible small back room which is full of clutter. Downstage right there is a stove where peat is burned and its smell suffuses the theatre space, without it being overwhelming or intrusive. Its mix and match furniture pieces form clusters of tables and chairs, and these offer a number of different drinking areas where the characters can congregate and also conjure distinct narrative spaces within the overall *mise-en-scène*. This layout of the furnishings also makes it possible for the characters to rotate regularly between these clusters of spaces. Such fluidity avoids any sense of a static or restrained performance sensibility.

Board games, a fire extinguisher, a box to collect money for religious missionaries, an electric fan, a bird cage and postcards all clutter the space. Behind the bar there is a calendar displaying April 1997. The back wall and centre stage serving area of the bar has a limited range of beer taps and alcoholic spirits on its shelves. Bacon fries, crisps, peanuts, and a small amount of domestic provisions are other design objects that define the characteristics of the space. (It seems as if its proprietor knows well the range and restricted tastes of his customers.) Additionally, an uneven range of drinking glasses compliments the seeming functionality and randomness of the other objects in the performance space.

In this production Ian Dickinson's subtle soundscape opts not for the boisterous windy conditions that are often very prominent in other productions of the work, but instead settles for something subtler and more gently evocative. Clearly, it is a world shaped by the rhythms of nature. These aural and scenographic specificities relate to, integrate with and accommodate Neil Austin's lighting design, whose primary use of golden and amber colours assist in making the atmosphere both one of warmth, welcome and potential foreboding. Also in many instances shadows are created as if to suggest that this is almost a spectral space, haunted as much by the associations, memories and losses implicit in the old photographs that adorn the walls, by the lingering energies of the pub's nightly customers, and by the moods and sensibilities of regularly narrated ghost stories. One could make out the details of some of the old photos on the walls, but others are not so clear. On these photos Rhona Trench notes:

> 'the ruined Abbey' is probably the remains of Jamestown Abbey—a Franciscan friary of the convent of the Friars' Minor from the seventeenth century, of 'the people posing near the ESB weir,' refers to the modern ESB weir at Jamestown built in 1951, which controls the

9 Tom Scutt, "Designing *The Weir*, see video http://www.donmarwarehouse.com/whats-on/donmar-warehouse/2013/the-weir.

> flow of water levels at that part of the river Shannon and which generates electric power, and 'a town in an alcove with mountains around it' which might be Drumshanbo, Co. Leitrim, surrounded by Sliabh an Iarainn which guards the south-eastern shore of Lough Allen, and the Arigna mountains. What the images capture have nothing to do with us, the audience, in terms of the original meaning of the events that surrounded them when they were taken. Instead, the audience will look at them and, based on their own lives, will infer meaning to them.[10]

Both the public and the private nature of these mementos illustrate the intermeshing of the domestic and the communal, the private and the collective to be found in this run-down bar that needs both de-cluttering and re-furbishing. Evoked by his design is a rural, isolated world caught between the general fantasy of sanctuary often associated with imagined west of Ireland spaces and the projected fantasies of metropolitan audiences as to what such pub environments suggest. As Nicholas Grene notes: 'Ireland is always available as a site for pastoral, in its greenness, its littleness, its location as the offshore-island alternative to the major metropolitan societies of Britain or America.'[11] Grene articulates the alignment of the pastoral with the 'archaic, traditional and originary', 'wholesome jollity' and 'harmony with nature'. He adds it is a space 'marked by quaintness, the charm, the lyrical otherness of Hiberno-English'.[12] (See also Terry Gifford's work.)[13]

Equally the play's pastoral comforting sensibility couples with the general public's familiarity with commercially designed, fey often kitsch Irish pubs that are to be found in many cities around the globe, where Irishness is enacted, transacted and substituted in an endless variety of ways. P.J. Mathews notes: 'Ironically, at the very moment in which the rural Irish pub was being replicated in abundance around the world, the same globalizing forces that promoted its popularity abroad were threatening the original of the species at home.'[14] Here in this play, Brendan's pub/bar serves as a symbol of a displaced home place, as centre for community interaction, as a hub for the sharing of information, and as a place to pass the time, drink and perhaps get inebriated. The pub bears the burden of uncertain communal memory, with the photographs on the walls stabilizing some of the memories of the past. Rather than being naturalistic, expressionistic or impressionistic, Scutt's scenography and Dickinson's lighting, and Austin's sound designs are notable for an intense

---

[10] Rhona Trench, 'The Measure of a Pub Spirit in Conor McPherson's *The Weir*' in Lilian Chambers and Eamonn Jordan eds., *The Theatre of Conor McPherson: Right Beside the Beyond* (Dublin: Carysfort Press, 2012), pp. 165-82, 173.

[11] Nicholas Grene, *The Politics of Irish Drama: Plays in Context from Boucicault to Friel* (Cambridge: Cambridge University Press, 1999), p. 212.

[12] Ibid., pp. 211-14.

[13] Terry Gifford, *Pastoral* (London: Routledge, 1999).

[14] P. J. Mathews, 'The "Sweet Smell" of the Celtic Tiger: Elegy and Critique in Conor McPherson's *The Weir*', in *The Theatre of Conor McPherson: Right Beside the Beyond*, pp. 151-64, 155.

level of detail, but the stage environment is established in ways that do not necessarily suggest a desire to embrace fully the notion of authenticity.

That said, plays set in such rural backwaters have faced strong criticism. Declan Hughes has voiced the most trenchant opinions, arguing that he 'could live a long and happy life without seeing another play set in a Connemara kitchen, or a country pub'. Hughes expresses his tiredness with work where there is an assumption of homogeneity, 'where everyone talks and thinks the same and holds values in common'. He even goes so far as to suggest that the village 'no longer signifies, doesn't resonate any more' on a mythological level. For him it is the 'spaces between cities' that carry such resonances, and stories that matter.[15] Clearly, McPherson draws on specific locations, yet also has the need to blur or disorientate things just a little. It is a heterotopic space in a Foucaultian sense.[16]

Acting the Part

With the exception of Brian Cox (Jack), Rourke uses four Irish actors, Risteárd Cooper (Finbar), Dervla Kirwan (Valerie), Ardal O'Hanlon (Jim), and Peter McDonald (Brendan).[17] From the off, Cooper as the rapscallion Finbar, appears comfortable, confident, suave, entrepreneurial and well groomed. He is the local character who has made good, who now lives in the nearby town of Carrick-on-Shannon and is in the hotel, property and auctioneering businesses – which coincidentally were many of the sectors that expanded most and were

---

[15] Declan Hughes, 'Reflections on Irish Theatre and Identity', in Eamonn Jordan ed., *Theatre Stuff: Critical Essays on Contemporary Irish Theatre* (Dublin: Carysfort Press, 2000), pp. 10-15, 11-13.

[16] See Michel Foucault, 'Of Other Spaces' trans. Jay Miskowiec. *Diacritics* 1.1 (Spring 1986), pp. 22-27.

[17] Only Cooper and Kirwan are new to McPherson's work as performers. Kirwan initially had made a name for herself in London in the early 1990s when she starred in Billy Roche's *A Handful of Stars*, and later in *The Wexford Trilogy* at the Bush Theatre, London. (Roche wrote the Programme note for this Donmar production, indeed Roche's and McPherson's friendship goes back a long way.) For many years Kirwan starred in *Ballykissangel*, and was the voice on many Marks and Spencer food advertisements - with the opening refrain 'This is not just food'. Cooper is best known as a successful and regularly cast actor at Dublin's Abbey and Gate Theatres and also for his work as a comedian and impressionist. Cox had performed in McPherson's work on previous occasions, starring in *St. Nicholas* (1997), *Dublin Carol* (2000) and in the film *Saltwater* (2000). O'Hanlon had already appeared in a production of *Port Authority* in 2012 at the Southwark Playhouse, London. McDonald has worked with McPherson on many occasions in the past. They had begun their careers on the student scene at University College Dublin's Dram Soc. He performed professionally in McPherson's *The Stars Lose Their Glory* at the International Bar, Dublin (1994) and also in 1994 in *Inventing Fortune's Wheel* at the Firken Crane Centre Cork (now Firkin Crane Theatre), and previously in the same play in 1992 in Dram Soc production. McDonald played Git Hynes in *I Went Down* (1997), which Paddy Breathnach directed, and McPherson wrote, and McDonald also starred in the National Theatre's production of *The Veil* (2011). (McDonald also wrote the Programme note for the premier of McPherson's *The Night Alive* [2013] at the Donmar Warehouse.)

worst hit by Ireland's economic collapse in late 2007.[18] Finbar claims to have a keen and speculative business sense or in his words 'an eye for the gap'. He is not entirely self-made, as he inherits much of his wealth from 'Big Finbar's will'.[19] According to Jack, Finbar's accrued capital is based on a mean streak, something that is neither affirmed nor denied by the play's dramaturgy. Finbar likes to display his wealth and intimidate others accordingly. As a married man with children, Finbar's personal motives for bringing Valerie to this backwater pub are multiple, complex and perhaps a little dubious. His offer to introduce Valerie to her neighbours does suggest a certain generosity, but his chaperoning or parading of her can be seen as a form of one-up-manship, as the other male characters in the play are relatively poor, have no children, and lack the intimacies, supports, benefits, pleasures, joys, compromises, sacrifices, complications and obligations of relationships. Equally, there is also a sense, given the kudos accruing to his indigenity and local knowledge that he may somehow be trying to entwine himself with Valerie's need to find comfort in rural isolation, and be identified or associated in some ways with the remoteness and sanctuary that she seemingly craves. In terms of status and allure, he can tick both the pastoral and urban or cosmopolitan boxes, even if it is small town, simultaneously and with ease. That said, Cooper's Finbar is not cast as the sexual predator and repulsive alpha male that he could potentially be. (Interestingly, of the four male actors, Cooper is the only one without a beard.)

Kirwan's Valerie is an outsider because of geography, background, and gender, and later maybe also because of the type of story she feels either free or compelled to tell in this predominantly male space: what is not made absolutely clear is which of these possibilities is the dominant one. Of the three actresses I have seen in the role, Kirwan demonstrates a serious uneasiness from the off, and, barely and convincingly disguises the events and impulses that have taken her to the west of Ireland, to leave her husband and family supports, to abandon Dublin and to purchase an isolated house in which she is determined to live alone. Despite that impulse towards isolation, she still finds herself in company, in this public house or liminal space that seems in some ways to be

[18] Based on textual evidence text critics are divided on this matter as to whether or not the play offers a consideration of the emergence of the Celtic Tiger (1993-2007). Helen Heusner Lojek notes 'McPherson's bar is not simply a synecdoche for Ireland–certainly not the Celtic Tiger so powerful in the early twenty-first century thinking about the island'. See *The Spaces of Irish Drama: Stage and Place in Contemporary Plays* (Basingstoke: Palgrave Macmillan, 2011), p.154. However, both Trench in 'The Measure of a pub spirit', pp.165-82 and Mathews in 'The Sweet Smell' associate the play very clearly with this Celtic Tiger period. While the purchase price for Valerie's house is not prohibitive, as Mathews argues, 'As it turned out, Leitrim and Sligo would subsequently experience huge levels of property speculation and development at the peak of the Celtic Tiger boom. Indeed, there is a dark irony, given the centrality of haunted houses in *The Weir*, that this region would inherit the unenviable title of 'ghost estates' capital of Ireland in the post-boom period'. pp.151-65.

[19] Conor McPherson, *The Weir* in *Plays: Two* (London: Nick Hern Books, 2004), pp. 26, 39, 26.

locked in a time warp, stuck in the 1950s or 1960s perhaps rather than being necessarily of her time. In many respects, the pub environment takes her outside of a recognizable time and out of a discernible space and into a different sensibility or rival consciousness. Kirwan embraces these various contradictory states of mind and surrenders her character to the potentials and consolations of this isolated, almost abandoned space.

Later the discovery that she has split from her husband, prompted by the unbearable grief of losing a daughter, Niamh, explains some of her early unease. Neither partner could protect, console nor bolster the other. It is a trauma that for her cannot be comforted by those who are close, familiar and proximate. Without an actor equipped to perform and acknowledge such emotional complexities, this play could struggle. To Kirwan's credit she keeps these anxieties and grief ever present with incredible, subtle focus, even as she at times nervously and cautiously laughs off the inadequacies of the bar's facilities – with no women's toilet functioning, and no chilled white wine to hand – however ludicrous these absences and omissions may be in functioning of public houses in the Ireland of that time. She demonstrates a degree of tolerance and a lessening of expectation that makes her less intimidating for those around her. Later, Kirwan's laughter becomes less self-conscious and less an expression of her politeness or cordiality: the nature of her laughter has a striking and notable evolution throughout Rourke's production as it progresses to become fundamentally participative, but not necessarily gender subversive. When Kirwan moves between the discrete narrative or performance spaces of the other characters, she is almost like a spectator moving between locations in an intimate site-specific piece of work. Indeed her transgressive mobility is choreographed to challenge the vectors and dynamics of this space and its possibly and rudimentary oppressive dispositions. Later, when Valerie tells her own story, she is laying claim to her own distinctive narrative space, but it also rounds the play in ways that are unnerving, harrowing and uncomfortable for the other characters that witness her story. Her space by the stove, downstage right, is not only the dominant stage space, but it also becomes a shared, collective space, yet it is clearly not the alignment of the feminine with the hearth or home. By the play's end it is the environment into which Brendan is drawn from his usual habitat that is from behind the bar.

Of the males, O'Hanlon's Jim is consistently on edge, embarrassed, stammering, eager and a little fixated on Valerie's presence, in ways that men that are not regularly in contact with the opposite sex can sometimes be. His passive qualities are echoed by the inexpensive polyester jumper, scruffy trousers and dirty boots that he wears, which of course contrast sharply with Finbar's sophisticated, urbane, casual attire or cream jacket and trousers and brown leather shoes. O'Hanlon illustrates his character's tacit understanding of his social status, and demonstrates a humility and a lack of resentment in the instance when the others skip over his turn to buy a round of drinks, which is of course an unspoken acknowledgement of his straightened financial circumstances.

Upon entering the empty pub, and seeing no bar person present, Cox's Jack is at liberty to serve himself a drink, and then unhurriedly, casually and confidently does so. Initially, the beer tap does not work, and Cox incorporates a great deal of humorous stage business into his performance, coaxing audience laughter. With an exorbitant gesture, Cox then checks a price list, opens the till and pays for his alcohol. These moments of self-service and payment not only set out the communal and pastoral tones of this play, but, also allow the spectator to grasp instantly some of the functional dynamics of this rural micro-community, mainly because Jack's actions are so much at odds with all customer transactions in 2013 in pubs around the Donmar Warehouse close by to Covent Garden, as they would have been in 1997 in the vicinity of Sloane Square when the play premiered there at the Royal Court. Indeed, there would have been very few public houses in Ireland even in the 1990s where such a transaction could have taken place. But actions like this did and still do happen in some rural communities in their shops and public houses. However, it would be naive to think that it is a communal sensibility based simply on collective trust, something innately noble, or a marker of mutual respect, as it may also have as much to do with mutual fear, the prospect of retaliation or the reporting of dishonesty to others and reputational damage that would ensue. Regardless, it still flags a form of trust that is made strange by its fundamental difference from liberal capitalist business norms, where transactions with customers are predominantly shaped by security tags, surveillance, suspicion, and regulation, therefore a fundamental absence of trust.

This predominant sensibility of mutuality is also evident throughout the play in the free drink that Brendan later hands over to Jim on his way home, and in the fact that Brendan's attitude towards his business seems to be based more on companionship and conversation and less about a desire to make a significant profit from the drinking habits of his customers. It is not so much that it is not-for-profit business per se, but Brendan's farming activities appear to be his main source of income. When the pub is busy with tourists, Brendan is disgruntled rather than excited by the additional revenues.

While there is something romantically civil, even innocent or naive in the customer arrangement which opens the play, it does not necessarily mean that the banter which follows is mutually cooperative, free from the pulling of rank or is naively romantic or utopian in perspective. The ensemble convincingly handles the edgy, jibing and competitive small talk that is evident throughout the early and relatively convivial introductions, but when it is time for the characters to avoid conversation or contentious debate, they do what Irish people in pubs often do best – and I hope I have not been too reductive here - that is tell stories. Now the play's register shifts, repelling the assumptions and conventions of naturalism and deliberately springboarding into another dimension, where the real, the imagined and the supernatural interface.

Finbar encourages Jack to tell a ghost story about fairies, fairy roads and encounters with the uncanny that occurred in Maura Nealon's old-home and Valerie's new abode. Surprisingly, in Cox's delivery there are very few brief pauses or delicate hesitations and there is often a slightly strained uncertainty in the telling, but what is especially striking is the speed at which he delivers the story. There is also no clear sense as to why he is telling this story in the first place. Cox's performance has a routinized, almost aggressive bluster to it, and his Jack is generally more of a trickster-like figure: different from how one might imagine him to be, his is a stronger, more assured, even a predatorial presence. Cox's Jack seems comfortable as rival to the younger men in the room, despite the fact that Cooper's Finbar, O'Hanlon's Jim and McDonald's Brendan are far closer in age to Kirwan's Valerie.[20] (My one criticism of Cox's exceptional performance is that on the day I saw the production, his accent is initially all over the place, but after a minute or so, he grounds it so successfully that one does not think about his accent again.)

Kirwan's Valerie remains relatively controlled, but modestly self-conscious throughout Jack's first narrative. She appears most aware that the house at the centre of Jack's story is the one that she has just purchased. The more the story progresses, Valerie is increasingly being reminded of her own paranormal encounters, whilst the males are effectively oblivious to the complex and fuller impact of Jack's story on her. Equally perhaps, Finbar's prompting of Jack to tell this story is not an innocent mistake: it is as if he wants Valerie to be a little unnerved by this story and her new surroundings. It also might be deduced that he may hope that Valerie might not want to be alone in her bed on this particular night. The way that Cooper scrutinizes Kirwan's reactions to the opening story makes this interpretation plausible.

Jack's initial narrative prompts Finbar to tell another story that involves the macabre, ghosts, Ouija boards, during an evening of events that prompted his moving away from the locality. Again, it is narrated with that strange pace I mentioned earlier. It is not made clear as to whether or not Finbar's motivation is to trump Jack, to put Valerie under additional pressure or that he truly believes in what he is saying. From a performance point of view, this is the right thing to do, that is, to keep ambivalence to the fore. Kirwan's Valerie is further unnerved by Jim's telling of a different type of story, about the supposed appearance of a dead man who requests to be buried not in his own grave but in that of a young girl's. While the delivery remains at the same high tempo as that of the two previous stories, what now surprises is how emotionally intense O'Hanlon's Jim becomes, as does his longing for Valerie's attention.

A Shot in the Dark

If three out of the four male characters have had their narrative opportunity or performance turn, Valerie effectively demands the next shot, and it is then that Kirwan's performance becomes even more impressive. Most surprising perhaps

[20] In contrast, when Jim Norton performed the role of Jack for the play's premiere, he took considerable glee in the invitation to deliver his first story. It was a declarative, sumptuous and expressive delivery of the tale, and he showed considerable delight in his own familiarity with and mastery of the environment through local knowledge. On this occasion, it was as if Norton delighted in the opportunity to add further flamboyance to a nightly routine once he had an additional spectator and a stranger in attendance.

is the fact that Valerie's narrative about the drowning of her daughter remains driven by the same pressured and speedy delivery mode as already mentioned in relation to the previous stories. This approach initially feels strange, even more than a little unnerving, in that it is out of sync with what most might expect to be the narrative rhythms of such sorts of deeply personal revelations, in terms of the emotions, intensities, silences, hesitations and tears, but her strange passion, almost a fixation, emerges through this very urgency. It becomes clear that the intention behind Rourke's pacing of the narratives is to veer away from easy associations and expectations spectators may have with real and supernatural narratives, skewing a natural empathetic response in many respects. Kirwan's performance is especially rigorous and accomplished in meeting such aspirations.

Throughout Kirwan's narrative I was especially attentive, as I had previously written that given the many overlaps and consistencies between Valerie's story and those that came before hers, it was possible to read her narrative as a ruse, as a clever deconstructive attack on the male characters' struggles for self-definition and the hold that they had over both the space and the storytelling format itself.[21] I made this argument based on the slight variation and repetition of many key words, names and concepts in her story that are in the previous three narratives. This was an idea inspired by McPherson's general indebtedness to a trickster sensibility evident in David Mamet's dramaturgy and approach to screen writing and by Bryan Singer's *The Usual Suspects* (1995), where Kevin Spacey's character Verbal Kint constructs a story based on fragments of details that come within his sight in a police station as he faces interrogation in the aftermath of a bloodbath on a ship. Comments by McPherson in a Preface to two of his plays about the conventions of telling stories in pubs substantiated that argument, as to whether or not something was true or fabricated did not matter so much on those occasions.[22]

Despite the skewed pacing, Kirwan's narrative captures the kernel of the traumatic experience at the death of her daughter, with not too much by way of emphasis on that meta-theatrical dimension or on the trickster embellishments and indicators that I have previously identified. That said, it seems clear that Kirwan does give particular emphasis to certain key words that are common across the stories, as if to underscore the repetitions, but to what ends I cannot be sure. And although disconcerted, Kirwan does take a certain delight in trumping the stories told by the others. It leaves the male characters prompting each other to assuage her anxieties and scrambling to provide rational explanations for some of the incidents that she has experienced and accounted for. Rourke's production particularly foregrounds the humiliation that the male characters variously appear to display in the aftermath of Valerie's narrative. Further, it is as if the energy and conviction of her story effectively break up the gathering. Finbar is sent home alone, so to speak.

---

[21] See Jordan, 'Pastoral Exhibits', pp. 351-68.

[22] Conor McPherson, 'Preface', *St. Nicholas* and *The Weir* (Dublin and London: New Island Books and Nick Hern Books, 1997), p. 32.

It is also telling that Kirwan's character confidently exerts a growing influence over the space. Her narrative enables her to heighten her status, but not in a way that is fundamentally threatening to the others. Evidence of this is seen in how Jack encourages her to protect herself from their nonsense talk. Her story also prompts Jack's telling of his own intimate story of love, lust, failure to commit and loss. It is at this point in the performance when Cox comes into his own. Firstly, Jack admits that the over-whelming sadness and humiliation he feels after the marriage ceremony of his exgirlfriend to a Dublin based policeman is utterly contrary to what he had expected to feel. Secondly, the consolation and generosity offered by a stranger, a bar man in a Dublin pub, stands out in his mind. Thirdly, while it is a 'real' story of sorts, it is also predominantly a ghost story, as he is haunted by his own cussedness, his own frailties, poor judgment and ultimately his lack of courage. Unlike in McPherson's latest work *The Night Alive* (2013) where Uncle Maurice (Jim Norton in another McPherson role) expresses the idea that one may only get two or three chances in life to get things right, here in the instance of *The Weir* second chances are not plentiful, and in a way the paucity of lifetime opportunities additionally marks the work as both uncanny and outside time.

Jack's story is delivered with great poignancy by Cox, but also with a little more aggression than Jim Norton brought to his performance at the Gate Theatre in 1998. With Norton I felt as if he was attempting to identify with Valerie's loss (Michelle Fairley), whereas with Cox there appears to be that empathy, but also it seems driven by a slender plea for Valerie to recognize him as an aging, but still sexually functional male. The details of him sleeping with his ex-girlfriend are laced with such a conviction. Jack's mood veers towards self-pity, but it is quickly abandoned thanks to levity and self-awareness. Even if this shared moment marks a fundamental hurt in his life, it is steered both by distancing techniques and also by the framing of loss in terms of a broader cosmic insignificance.

Of course, the evening's master of ceremonies has been McDonald's Brendan, another lonesome and youngish enough bachelor. McDonald has a terrific comic ability to combine reticence, introverted vulnerability and self-conscious, playful emotion, and he is capable of delivering it in a throw-away fashion. Although Brendan has no story of any sort to tell, McDonald's interactions throughout with Kirwan's Valerie are impressively subtle, especially as the play concludes. As Valerie sits by the stove, Brendan moves over to join her. There is a hesitant and heightened sexual tension acknowledged between both characters. The tentative bond between them both at this moment is neither simplistic nor a soppy futuristic signalling of a happy-ever-after type scenario. As Rourke stages it, it is an encounter between them that is prompted by the courage to be open to the possibility of connection with others and not by a naive optimism. Out of the mire of debilitating consciousnesses and inhibiting, past-orientated narratives, it is now a drama tentatively affirming the present and a future with possibilities.

In one telling moment after Valerie kindly locates Brendan's missing keys, the textual suggestiveness of such a gesture is clearly foregrounded by Kirwan's flirtatious demeanour. Soon after McDonald is convincing in capturing his character's now more relaxed mode of being, when talking carelessly about Valerie's attractiveness to Finbar, stating: 'He'll be like a fly on a big pile of shite'.[23] To McDonald's credit he makes this unfortunate turn of phrase seem less like an expression of rudeness or frankness, and less again like an indication of a process of normalizing her objectivization, but more like him being less guarded and freer in her company. Alcohol helps in that regard. There is a certain charm and comfort in Brendan's status as the beta to Finbar's misguided aspirations to be the alpha male of the night's gathering.

In the 1980s and 1990s in particular, it was in vogue to view the gender politics of any piece of work regarded as close to naturalism as being regressive, conformist, conventional and active in the circulation of patriarchal imperatives.[24] With the exception of Finbar, the general status, 'honour, prestige', 'the right to command' and the 'material' gains that R.W. Connell associates with the dividends of patriarchy that accrue to men are clearly not realized here in this play.[25] Anything but a trivial alignment of the male characters in the reproduction and dissemination of patriarchy seems like a reductive response to the work.[26] In the relative circumstances of their lives, the dividends of patriarchy are almost notional to the likes of Jim and Jack. Valerie is the character that is most articulate, grounded and mobile and she can partake as an equal in the 'metaphysical debate' as well as having equal purchase on the imaginative/supernatural spheres.[27]

Helen Heusner Lojek notes of the dramatic space in this play that: 'it is a warm, private space in which individuals can and do come together, because of and regardless of exterior realities: a retreat separate from the world of work, a place where drinkers meet with a degree of equality that may not be found outside the bar.'[28] And in many ways not only is this equality a temporary issue, but more importantly it functions in ways to contest the relatively fixed structures of inequality that are a global reality. In fact, what Rourke's production clearly foregrounds is that the socially and politically marginalized is not just female specific, there is a strong class basis to it. The production does not mask the inequalities of elsewhere, rather it foregrounds them and also

---

[23] Conor McPherson, *The Weir*, p. 73.

[24] While there are four male characters to one female performer in this work, other female figures also enter the psychic landscape, even if they are predominantly filtered through a male frame, namely, Maura Nealon, Niamh Walsh, Jim's mother, Brendan's scheming sisters, and the accounts of cheating wives tidying bed linen after sex in hotel rooms, and of course Valerie's daughter Niamh.

[25] R.W. Connell, 'The Social Organisation of Masculinity', in Stephen M. Whitehead and Frank Barrett eds., *The Masculinities Reader* (Cambridge: Polity Press, 2001), pp. 30-50, 40-43.

[26] In the Irish tradition of theatre writing there is a reluctance to talk about or deal with money issues in any comprehensive way. McPherson's work does not follow that trend.

[27] Lynda Henderson, 'Men, Women and the Life of the Spirit in Tom Murphy's Plays' in Jacqueline Genet and Wynne Hellegoarc'h eds., *Irish Writers and Their Creative Process* (Gerrards Cross: Colin Smythe, 1996), pp. 87-89, 88-90.

[28] Helen Heusner Lojek, *The Spaces of Irish Drama*, pp. 59-60.

reveals the bias and romance that metropolitan centres always have had for that which is marginalized. In the pub space, there are male and female characters, unafraid of their status and differences as men and women, with different experiences, backgrounds and occupations, who gain some access to the potential dividends of interrelating and sharing.

Based on work by Richard Shweder and Jonathan Haidt, anthropologist Alan Fiske devised a taxonomy of relationality, which Steven Pinker alters slightly. Fiske's model emphasizes 'Communal Sharing' – based on in-group loyalty, bonding and rituals of togetherness. It is a bonding based on care and protection. The second is 'Authority Ranking' – based on dominance, status, precedents, etc. The dominant figures take what they need and demand loyalty and in return they offer protection and assurances. The third model is 'Equality Matching,' something which 'embraces tit-for-tat reciprocity and other schemes to divide resources' as equitably and as fairly as possible. Fiske's final relational model is 'Market Pricing,' and this is about money, and financial value, and is not nearly as universal.[29] Thus Pinker substitutes the term 'Rational-Legal' as his final model.[30] This taxonomy thus provides a 'grammar for social norms'.[31] To be a 'socially competent member of a culture is to have assimilated a large set of these norms'.[32]

In a different publication, Pinker reminds us that in evolutionary terms the 'Rational-legal' or capitalism model is a relatively new one,[33] With his not-for - profit pub and with the emphasis given to communal sharing throughout this play, McPherson brings on board forms of 'reciprocal altruism', a 'logic of *reciprocity',* even an 'ethos of reciprocity' to use Pinker's evolutionary psychology terminology.[34] McPherson is effectively challenging the dominance of the liberal capitalist model, and suggests that there are other equally valid forms of relating.

In Rourke's production, almost everything is as seamless and coherent as one would ideally want it to be. There are trivial exceptions. For instance, despite all of the great strengths that O'Hanlon possesses as a performer, including a wonderful illuminating presence on stage, plus an ability to reflexively lower status as the situation requires, at times, the stage seems like an unnatural, uncomfortable environment for him, particularly, when he does

---

[29] Steven Pinker, *The Better Angels of Our Nature: A History of Violence and Humanity* (London: Penguin Books, 2011), pp.756-58.

[30] While each of these modes of relating can have positive outcomes, they also have potentially negative ones as well. Communal sharing has a tendency to exclude out-groups, 'legitimise tribalism and jingoism' and only serves the needs of those close to hand and affiliated. Authority Ranking justifies authority way beyond paternalism. Imperialists, slave owners and despots have their own logical application of authority to themselves. Equality Matching provides a justification for retaliation in relationships, the rationale for Rational-Legal model can be used to justify major global inequalities. Ibid., pp.766-69.

[31] Ibid., p.759.

[32] Ibid., p.760.

[33] Steven Pinker, *The Blank Slate*: *The Modern Denial of Human Nature* (London: Penguin, 2002), p.234.

[34] Ibid., p. 255-56.

awkwardness awkwardly. The telling of his story is one of the few times that this does not appear to be the case, and maybe that is because he is obliged to be relatively still while delivering his narrative.[35] Additionally, although Cooper brings an endearing quality to his role as Finbar, in part Finbar is played more often to be laughed at, and this thus entices less a laughter of self or collective recognition on behalf of the spectator and more one of condescension towards this character.

Equally, Cooper's Finbar is a fundamentally confused character, further befuddled by some of the choices made by him or for him in this production. That said, Cooper delivers his supernatural narrative with exceptionally uncanny inflections and with a distanced, glazed intensity. These critiques of the two performances are slight and do not amount to substantial production frailties. Indeed such flaws are utterly offset by the consistently astonishing performances delivered by Cox, Kirwan and McDonald.

By using multiple bar room tables around which to cluster figuratively her characters, by energizing the space with a great deal of physical action, Rourke extracts far more humour from the work than I remember from the other performances of this play that I have seen previously. This comedy is seen in either the exaggerated cantankerousness of Cox's Jack's self-defence mechanisms or in the gentle gestural comedy of the piece, evident in the instance when Brendan pours Valerie's un-chilled white wine into a half-pint glass and fills it up to the brim.

In this production there is also a great alertness to the tragi-comic sensibility that drives dialectical character oppositions, that are not only between characters but are also played as tensions within characters: the simultaneities that exist between frailty and resilience, surrender and persistence, and between denial and obstinacy are cleverly incorporated, as each actor demonstrates complexities that are harmonized and counter-balanced by an array of rival impulses.

In the networks of relationships established between these characters, Rourke affirms a circularity rather than a linearity of time, and an inter-digitation of different sorts of spaces, namely fictional, personal, supernatural, contrived ones. It is not simply to wonder if a supernatural world exits, but it is more about what 'shadows' existence; an awareness of twin or multiple worlds to which dreamscapes can give one access. A drugged and sedated Valerie could imagine or hallucinate anything, including phone calls from her dead daughter. Jim also explains the supernatural through fever and an alcoholic haze. The thin line between the personal experience narrated and the supernatural is crossed with great regularity, often apologetically, but the frequency with which it happens proves the uncertainty and the need. There is also the comfort of stories. Richard Kearney suggests that 'Telling stories is as basic to human beings as eating. More so, in fact, for while food makes us live, stories are what

[35] In 2014 O'Hanlon was nominated for an Olivier Award for best actor in a supporting role.

make our lives worth living. They are what make our condition *human*'.[36] He adds that it is the art of storytelling that 'gives us a shareable world'.[37] In performing, articulating, listening and witnessing, the play's narrative encounters mark out the need to give form and coherence to the chaos of being, and the performances in this production do likewise with a brilliant ease.

However, there are also further questions stoked by Enda Walsh's query: 'I'm defined by five stories to my brothers. I know they know me through these stories and I know my brother John through four stories, and that is enough for us ... We're blood, it's enough for us, it is our church, our mass, our kitchen at home ... But what if these stories are not real, if they are actually lies, or when do they stop being real?'[38] This raises not only the extent of narrative fabrication, but that identities formatted on such narratives can result in all kinds of illusions and consequences for subjectivity. Across *The Weir*, some stories are accepted, rubbished, queried, and taken at face value for the embellishments therein. Brendan's sisters may dine together in order to get a story straight before they meet him, local history can be an invention, and communal memories are sometimes held in focus only by photographs on the wall, and vague associations with them.

Classic Status

When given the type of treatment and commitment that it gets from Rourke's direction, the designers, and her ensemble of actors, this production confirms *The Weir*'s classic status, and also affirms that responsive audiences, very positive critical responses by reviewers and those that handed out awards to this work's first production in 1997 did get its significance and substance right. This wonderfully coherent production captures the banter, disguised intimidation, and regulated and faux aggression that are offset by bonhomie, and an openness and generosity of spirit. It is a theatrical world not so much saturated by stories but one situated betwixt and 'between' stories, to vary Hughes's notion of in-betweenness. In the fundamental need to attest a story, to share it, and to witness it, the characters put themselves at the mercy of each other and at the mercy of an ensemble of relative strangers in the theatre, sitting and experiencing the potential of otherness.

McPherson clearly writes predominantly from a sensibility of fear and responses to it, while hovering relentlessly are issues of chaos, abandonment, inability to connect or fear of one's own darker desires. It is a dramaturgy that offers a poetics of tentativeness and dis-ease, rather than straightforward abjection or terror, and serves to prioritize the small joys and playful humour in character interaction, rather than potentially satirical and aggressive engagements founded on subtextual currents of anger, rivalries, resistance and

[36] Richard Kearney, *On Stories* (London: Routledge, 2002), p. 3.
[37] Ibid.
[38] Enda Walsh, 'Interview' http://www.stannswarehouse.org/enda_interview.html.

hostility. There remains ever-present the potential for 'grace'[39] and 'communion',[40] for this provisional community of characters, imagined and consolidated as different. Rourke's *mise-en-scène* matches this sensibility.

Bruce McConachie explains how in either real life or through experiencing a performance on stage our neurological responses or mirror neurons can be triggered, as we engage with genres, sounds, rhythms, moods, movements and emotions, visual and aural clues.[41] Indeed such mirroring can be contagious for spectators. He identifies the significant impact of movement and sound on 'spectatorial empathy' in particular.[42] One of the great strengths of *The Weir* is the huge range of emotions it churns over, and responses it entices. More importantly, it is often that which is denied, concealed, repressed, subtextual or kept at a distance is more important than what is displayed, which has the most impact on the responses and engagements of spectator. (See Steven Pinker for a counter argument on empathy and mirror neurons).[43]

While productions of any single dramatic text vary considerably, there are certain fundamentals, sequences, causalities and continuities that cannot be avoided, and in that way, acts of critical engagement cannot be served by the notion of surrogation at all. But criticism is an act of embodied engagement, investment of presence, shaped endlessly by attitudes, values, prejudice, distractedness, concentration, and random thoughts, where the essential and what is incidental run rival and simultaneous systems.[44] But I would not go so far as to suggest that it is some 'incommensurable' act of transformation, as Worthen sees the relationship between text and performance. While almost all critical responses to this play are different, most seem to be struggling to deal with the same issues such as place, money, narrative, time and gender. And from my own responses to this current performance, there is the realization just how much one brings of one's own history and experiences, one's conversations, one's teaching, one's writing, one's reactions to critical commentary and how one's responses to a performance are often shadowed by experiences of previous productions. There can be problems with being over-familiar with a work, less emotionally engaged, less easily instinctive and also perhaps overly anticipative in one's responses.

Criticism is almost always an act of self-confrontation, of allowing the conscious and unconscious mind, memory and knowledge to interface creatively and imaginatively in the intensity of the moment. This article also illustrates how much Rourke's production affirms, reinforces, tempers and

[39] Kevin Kerrane, 'The Structural Elegance of Conor McPherson's *The Weir*,' *New Hibernia Review*, 10: 4 (2006), pp. 105-21, 121.

[40] Helen Heusner Lojek, *The Spaces of Irish Drama*, p. 63.

[41] Bruce McConachie, *Engaging Audiences*, pp. 67-72.

[42] Ibid., p. 71.

[43] Steven Pinker, *The Better Angels of Our Nature*, pp. 696-99.

[44] Even on the day I saw this production I was struck by a snapshot memory of the day I drove through Jamestown, once the home to McPherson's deceased grandfather, and how underwhelming was my response to seeing the local weir, constructed by the Electrical Supply Board (ESB) on the river Shannon.

challenges my own ideas about and previous responses to this play by McPherson.

EAMONN JORDAN is a Senior Lecturer in Drama Studies at University College Dublin. He is the author of numerous critical essays on Irish dramatists, such as Marie Jones, Martin McDonagh, Conor McPherson, and Enda Walsh. He edited *Theatre Stuff: Critical Essays on Contemporary Irish Theatre* in 2000. He co-edited with Lilian Chambers *The Theatre of Martin McDonagh: A World of Savage Stories* (2006) and *The Theatre of Conor McPherson: 'Right beside the Beyond'* (2012). He has written three monographs *The Feast of Famine: Plays of Frank McGuinness* (1997), *Dissident Dramaturgies: Contemporary Irish Theatre* (2010) and *From Leenane to LA: The Theatre and Cinema of Martin McDonagh* (2014).

Gay Masculinities in Performance: Towards a Queer Dramaturgy

CORMAC O'BRIEN

[This essay interrogates correlations between gay masculinities in performance, the dramaturgical contexts and strategies within which they are performed, and the socio-political and cultural praxes of neoliberal ideologies. Charting recent shifts in performances of gay masculinities in Irish theatre, identified broadly as a move from gay dramas into queer theatre, the essay argues that this performative trajectory signals a dramaturgical resistance against an assimilatory, neoliberal, gay male homogeneity, identified by several queer theorists as 'homonormativity', within the broader LGBT culture. This essay analyses the ways in which current Irish queer theatre practitioners mobilize labile, fragmented, non-linear dramaturgical strategies to situate the spectator within a wide gamut of still-forming, non-hierarchal subjectivities, which thus lends itself to the realities of gay masculine subjectivities as they are moved and shaped by – and rail against – heteronormative culture.]

Much progress has been made in terms of gay visibility and the quelling of homophobia in Irish society and cultural productions since the decriminalization of homosexuality in the Republic in 1993.[1] Remarkably, however, the constitutional legitimization and cultural acceptance of gay citizenship occurred in tandem with the rise of Ireland's economic boom, the Celtic Tiger – an era which saw the deep entrenchment of many neoliberal political policies and cultural practices that continue unabated, despite the global economic crash of 2008 and its subsequent long recession.

[1] Homosexual sex acts between men in the Republic of Ireland were, after a long political and activist struggle involving the European Court of Human Rights, decriminalized in 1993. The most indepth analysis is Kieran Rose, *Diverse Communities: The Evolution of Lesbian and Gay Politics in Ireland* (Cork: Cork University Press, 1994).

Neoliberalism, as Colin Crouch defines it, has 'many branches and brands'. However, Crouch continues,

> behind them stands one dominant theme: that free markets in which individuals maximise their material interests provide the best means for satisfying human aspirations, and that markets are in particular to be preferred over states and politics, which are at best inefficient and at worst threats to freedom.

In neoliberal societies, therefore, where markets do not exist they must be created, and in service of those markets, so too must citizenship be reformulated as 'consumership'.

Neoliberalism's championing of markets and creation of hyper-consumers means that, in cultural productions, media events, and, crucially, in dramatic representations onstage and onscreen, only the most profitable depictions of gender and sexuality prevail. Ubiquitous in Western gay cultures, therefore, is a commodified, idealized gay masculinity, or what Sharif Mowlabocus calls an 'homogenizing gay aesthetic'.[2] With its emphasis on young, muscled, corporeal perfection, this gay aesthetic promotes and is enabled by aspirational, middle-class affluence that can financially afford plush private residences and high-end leisure activities. Neoliberal cultural practices thus sanction gay masculine visibility strictly in terms of happy, apolitical, hyper-consumers who can easily emulate heterosexual consumerism and lifestyles thereby, as Dana Collins argues, 'impl[ying] that the reality of gay life is positive, or at least coherent enough to be represented, which presents a dilemma for those who intentionally use representation politically.'[3]

This essay explores the correlations between gay masculinities in performance, the dramaturgical contexts and strategies within which they are performed, and the socio-political and cultural praxes of neoliberal ideologies. I argue that there has been a recent shift in performances of gay masculinities in Irish theatrical culture, which I identify broadly as a move from gay dramas into queer theatre. This shift is distinguishable by the dramaturgical strategies mobilized by queer theatre makers as they disavow realist, narrative drama in favour of radical, free-flowing theatrical forms and structures, in an effort to resist the commodification of gay male identities and the apolitical assimilation of gay lives and living into mainstream heterosexual socio-economic and cultural structures.

The performative trajectory that gay masculinities in Irish theatre have followed, particularly in the last decade, thus signals a dramaturgical resistance against this assimilatory, gay male homogeneity: an homogeneity that queer theorists such as Collins and Michael Warner call 'homonormativity'. Tapping into a nascent zeitgeist of queer masculinities in performance that, through a

---

[2] Sharif Mowlabocus, 'Gay Men and the Pornification of Everyday Life' in Susanna Paasonen, Kaarina Nikunen & Laura Saarenmaa, eds., *Pornification: Sex and Sexuality in Media Culture* (Oxford: Berg, 2007), pp. 67-48, p. 67.

[3] Dana Collins, 'No Experts Guaranteed!: Do-It-Yourself Sex Radicalism and the Production of the Lesbian Sex Zine "Brat Attact",'*Signs*, 25:1 (1999), pp. 65-89. p. 65.

recalibration of traditional realist dramaturgy, politically challenge neoliberal formulations of hyper-consumer 'happy gays', this essay argues that such a reinvigorated, experiential dramaturgy explores individuated queer masculine subjectivities at both political and quotidian levels.

Realism and its Discontents

Loughlin Deegan's play *The Queen and Peacock* (2000) dramatizes the coming out story of Paul, a gay Irishman living in London. Set in a backstreet Brixton pub, the eponymous Queen and Peacock, the play subscribes to the entrenched Irish tradition of realist narrative drama, not least in its barroom setting but more so with its cause and effect progress towards cathartic resolution. The drama opens with bitchy drag-queen and sex-worker Gertie, aka Mark, dancing to the jukebox. Gertie's latest pick-up, Willie, a nineteen-year-old and very macho lad – what Raewyn Connell would call 'a very straight gay'[4] – who has newly arrived from Dublin, plays the fruit machine. Behind the bar, Bob, the licensee, cleans glasses while attempting to keep the drunken Gertie in check. When Paul, the main protagonist, enters, he is extremely troubled because their friend, Ciarán, another gay Irishman and offstage character, is dying from an AIDS-related illness in a nearby hospice.

Neither Bob nor Gertie seems to care about Ciarán, despite his being a regular customer and part of their cohort. Gertie, moreover, identifies Paul's anxieties as running deeper than Ciarán's impending death. Paul is, according to Gertie, a 'Hiberno-Queer' – 'a particular breed of immigrant [...] in hiding [...] from their friends and their families and their friends and the prying eye of our good friend, Holy Catholic Ireland'.[5] And while Willie rebuts such easy stereotyping, citing the millennial Dublin he has just left behind as a liberal, gay-friendly city, Gertie's accusations of Paul ring true. Paul is deeply closeted, ashamed of his sexuality, and cannot bring himself to come out to his parents back in Donegal, despite their wanting him to return home and take early-inheritance of the thriving family pub due to his father's poor health.

However, Ciarán's death (during the interval) and Bob's revelation of the Queen and Peacock's unavoidable closure force Paul to re-evaluate his reasons for being in London. Spurred on by Willie's stories of a newly progressive Ireland and goaded by Gertie about his closeted-ness, Paul phones his parents in Donegal and tells them he is gay. As the final curtain falls, Willie sets off to find adventure in London's Soho, and Paul makes plans to return home triumphant. Gertie, meanwhile, is left tragically alone, not knowing where to go or what to do once the pub finally closes its doors. Thus Paul, the prodigal gay son, having undergone the supposed psychosexual healing offered by the confessional act of disclosing his sexual orientation, is rewarded with an easy return to Mother Ireland and the family business.

---

[4] R.W. Connell, *Masculinities* (Cambridge: Polity, 2005), p. 143.

[5] Loughlin Deegan, *The Queen and Peacock* in Fintan Walsh, ed., *Queer Notions: New Plays and Performances from Ireland* (Cork: Cork University Press, 2010), pp. 17-70, p. 29.

Eight years later, BrokenTalkers show *Silver Stars* (2008) presents more complex and realistic interrogations of Irish gay masculinities by, paradoxically, breaking away from realist dramatic narrative altogether. Billed as 'a moving and eloquent song-cycle, which tells the truly extraordinary real-life stories of older gay Irishmen [...] in a country that was challenged by their very existence', *Silver Stars* was devised by its cast and directors, Feidlim Cannon and Gary Keegan, with songs and script by Sean Millar.[6] Eight song sequences are performed by ten men, many of whom are not professional actors. Sometimes solo, sometimes duet, each song has a chorus sung in unison by all ten men. Performed on a bare wooden floor, with cello players at the side of the stage, the songs are augmented by video footage of interviews and significant events from the history of Irish and American gay rights movements projected onto a large screen above the playing area.

Each song-sequence recounts a life of struggle and shame that was yet imbued with hope and pride. From the story of Aiden, whose mother travelled to visit him in Paris to tell him that 'my God has told me your life is a sin [...] I love you more than God', through the recorded interview of John, an ex-Jesuit priest, which is lip-synched by an actor wearing glasses with painted-on eyes, to video footage of queer activist protests against the banning of gay Irish-Americans from New York's St. Patrick's Day parade with an impassioned speech by Robert Rygor, a prominent Irish-American AIDS activist, *Silver Stars* conveys the need for gay masculine subjectivities to overcome deeply embedded belief systems that have long been the mainstay of Irish socio-cultural, political, and religious life. Yet these men do not deny Ireland, they want to be Irish – their songs perform the search for national identity despite state-sanctioned denial of citizenship. After Aiden's song, for example, all the men stand in triangular formation, each one displaying a photograph of his mother, foregrounding how both theatrical and social performances of gay masculinities disrupt the boundaries between the ostensibly private realms of family and intimacy, and the political arenas of LGBT rights and citizenship.

Silver Stars is thus an experiential theatre event, drawing the spectator into a plurality of gay masculine subjectivities and life-narratives as they struggle to reconcile queerness with nationhood. Its fragmentation of narrative and structure, floating imperceptibly from poignant solo voice to rousing emotive chorus, explores the structures of queer lives and the ways in which official discourses of Irishness mobilized gay-shaming in order to silence those lives. Thus the spectator is identified with and yet paradoxically sympathetic to, even apologetic for, a collective shaming of these ten lives, and, by extension, many thousands of others.

While *Queen and Peacock* can be considered a gay Irish drama, or a drama about gay Irishmen, *Silver Stars*, by contrast, operates as a queer performance or as Irish queer theatre. There are, of course, thematic strands linking both,

---

6 See BrokenTalkers' website, 'Silver Stars', (2008), http://www.brokentalkers.ie/, [accessed 19 December 2013]. There is no extant script for *Silver Stars*, Brokentalkers kindly provided a video of the performance.

not least in their explorations of coming out as a gay Irishman. Both share, as an overarching motif, a critique of an Ireland in which gay men have been shamed into silence, denied a sense of national belonging and, up until 1993, legal citizenship. And both speak, albeit in different ways, to the devastation that HIV and AIDS have wreaked on LGBT communities not just in Ireland and England, but also around the world.[7] Yet the ways in which *Queen and Peacock* and *Silver Stars* dramaturgically tackle these themes of social and familial shame, subjective disavowal, HIV/AIDS, and LGBT rights are vastly different.

Queer practice – and by this I mean theatre, scholarship, and activism (and the three are closely interrelated) – has always had as its central discourse a critique of what Warner identifies as 'regimes of the normal'.[8] Specifically, queer practice mobilizes against heteronormativity; the assumption that heterosexuality is not just the only socially acceptable mode of living and loving, but also that any counter-normative sexualities have 'deviated' from – are deviant to – heterosexuality and so, to function properly, must aspire to its paradigms, life narratives, and temporalities. As Sarah Ahmed asserts, 'heteronormativity refers to more than simply the presumption that it is normal to be heterosexual. The "norm" is regulative, and is supported by an "ideal" that associates sexual conduct with other forms of conduct.'[9]

Silver Stars, as a queer theatre event that interrogates the ways state-sanctioned and quotidian regulatory norms map across the political and the personal, mobilizes two key nodes of queer practice. First, it marshals performances of biopolitics – that meeting point between authoritarian politics and everyday life – by interrogating how political power is wielded over those bodies that have been medically, politically, and culturally pathologized as 'other' and 'dangerous' in order to control and sometimes eliminate them.[10] The second node of queer practice that *Silver Stars* rallies is Eve Sedgwick's confounding of the discursively created 'homo/hetero' binary. Sedgwick debunks the populist 'axiomatic' melding of queer sexual practices with other preconceived, non-sexual, but equally 'suspect' or 'abhorrent' behaviours in everyday life and lifestyles.[11] Hence, the men perform in plain, ordinary clothes, nondescript jeans and shirts, a muted beige suit, pointing to a visible absence of the stereotyped, soignée flamboyancy of so much gay-male costuming in Irish

---

7 It should be noted that *Queen and Peacock* anachronistically ignores the realities of living with HIV in the year 2000, a time by which antiretroviral treatments that halted the mass deaths of the AIDS 'crisis years' from 1981-96 were available, free of charge, to all HIV-positive persons living in Ireland and the UK, and had thus become imbricated within gay lives and culture.

8 Michael Warner, 'Introduction' in Michael Warner, ed., *Fear of a Queer Planet: Queer Politics and Social Theory* (Minneapolis: University of Minnesota Press, 1993), pp. vii-xxxi, p. xxxvi.

9 Sara Ahmed, 'Queer Feelings' in Donald E. Hall & Annamarie Jagose, eds., *The Routledge Queer Studies Reader* (Abingdon: Routledge, 2013), pp. 422-41, p. 427.

10 See, in particular, Michel Foucault's 'Right of Death and Power over Life' in Timothy Campbell & Adam Sitze, eds., *Biopolitics: A Reader* (Durham: Duke UP, 2013), pp. 41-60.

11 Eve Kosofsky Sedgwick, *Epistemology of the Closet* (Berkeley: University of California Press, 2008), pp. 1-63.

theatre (as exemplified by the character Rory in Rough Magic's April 2013 revival of Declan Hughes' *Digging for Fire* [1991]).[12] The performers' stance and movement too are imbued with the heavy gait of everyday workingmen; there are no flapping wrists, high-pitched voices, or giddy excitability. Indeed, they look like the personification of hegemonic masculinity. *Silver Stars* thus disrupts the heteronormative reification of 'the homosexual as a personage' or 'species'[13] – as a distinct type of personality that is always identified and identifiable by virtue of their choice of sexual partner. When these men sing their life-narratives their message is that while they are just ordinary men, their lives have been marked, sometimes ruined, by homophobic assumptions about their identities and biopolitical manipulations of their bodies.

Queen and Peacock, conversely, in banishing gay men to a backstreet pub, and separating them, by virtue of their sexuality, from the rest of society, not only reinforces the homo/hetero binary but is also uncritical of the biopolitics of hiding queer masculine bodies. Despite Deegan's assumed critique-by-depiction of such hiding, it still reinforces the 'them and us' of heterosexist ideologies. Moreover, in an effort to counter this hiding, Paul and Willie discover strategies by which their 'homosexual personage' can best assimilate into normative cultures. Simultaneously, the tragic figures of Gertie and the dead-from-AIDS Ciaran serve as cautionary tales regarding the dangers of non-assimilation.

Interrogating queer assimilation into heterosexual cultures, Ahmed argues that:

> Assimilation involves a desire to approximate an ideal that one has already failed; and identification with one's designation as a failed subject. The choice of assimilation – queer skin, straight masks – is clearly about supporting the violence of heteronormative distinctions between legitimate and illegitimate lives.[14]

Paul, by undergoing the psychic confessional of coming out, renders his illegitimate life legitimate; assimilation into normative culture assures him that he is not a failure. Whereas Gertie – who, according to Paul, is a 'bloody freak show [...] don't even know what it is to be normal' (43) – is punished with a lonely, ever-illegitimate life for his failure to enter normativity. Ciarán, who performed his queerness by dressing in rubber and cruising the sex clubs of London, and 'could have been a bit more selective about where he stuck his cock' (44), suffers the ultimate negation for his failure to emulate normativity. Shoring up what Anne Mulhall identifies as 'the phobic association between queerness and annihilation', Ciarán dies, offstage and unmet by the spectator, punished by that very convenient castigator of queerness in popular and

---

[12] Declan Hughes, *Digging For Fire* in *Declan Hughes: Plays 1* (London: Methuen Drama, 1998), pp. 1-75.

[13] Michel Foucault, *The Will to Knowledge: History of Sexuality 1* (London: Penguin, 1979), p. 43.

[14] Ahmed, p. 426.

theatrical culture – AIDS.[15] Willie, by virtue of his youthful good looks and hard-bodied 'straight-acting' homo-masculinity will easily assimilate into not only the body-conscious, commercialized gay scene of Soho, but can also walk undetected among the heterosexist society in which he will consequently thrive. Therefore, Paul manages entry into normativity *despite* his sexuality, and thus by assimilating can seek to overcome any challenges that being gay might present. Ultimately, queerness is presented as a sexuality that comes with a set of social problems that can only be overcome by emulating a heterosexual lifestyle.

The men of *Silver Stars*, conversely, by performing non-linear song-cycles of adverse life-narratives, question not only heternormativity, but more so the very concept of norms, and systems of theatrical and social normalizing such as realist narratives that lead to neat, cathartic conclusions by rewarding those who conform to regulatory norms, and punishing those who do not. Moreover, rather than just critique heteronormativity as a fixed state of being or living, the experiential dramaturgy of *Silver Stars* draws the spectator into the midst of lives that buck normative trends, thus foregrounding the ways in which adherence to any norm is an ongoing series of active processes to which bodies must subject themselves. Each song cycle's melding of the personal with the queer political exposes how social bodies are ideologically interpellated towards a continual rendering into normativity, a rendering that autologously galvanizes heteronormativity's need for perpetual reinforcing and refreshing. This kaleidoscope of polyphonic, polysemic performances highlights how, as Ahmed puts it, 'Heteronormativity involves the reproduction or transmission of culture through how one lives one's life in relation to others.'[16] The men in *Silver Stars* ask neither for franchise nor a place at the table of heteronormativity. Because, asking for assimilatory entry into heterosexist society is to state that queer masculinities need something outside of themselves to tell them what they are and dictate how they should function. In singing their stories the men of *Silver Stars* experientially inform the spectator that the reason their life-narratives have played out in these ways is because heteronormative society does not know how to deal with queerness other than to, eventually, and after many years of violent, state-sanctioned homophobia, offer it crumbs from the table of assimilation.

My comparative analysis of *Queen and Peacock* and *Silver Stars* makes clear the ideological links between gay assimilation into neoliberal, heteronormative cultures, and the ways in which queer masculine subjectivities

[15] Anne Mulhall, 'Introduction: Queering the Issue,' *Irish University Review: Special Edition, Queering the Issue*, 43:1 (2013), pp. 1-11, p. 1. Mulhall draws from a strand in queer theory that interrogates populist associations of queerness with death, most recently theorized by Lee Edelman, in *No Future: Queer Theory and the Death Drive*' (Duke University Press, 2004). For analyses of how AIDS galvanizes populist linkage of queerness with death, see Leo Bersani, 'Is the Rectum a Grave,' *October*, 43 (1987), pp. 197-222; Jeff Nunokawa, 'All the Sad Young Men', and Ellis Hanson, 'Undead' in Diana Fuss, ed., *Inside Out: Lesbian Theories, Gay Theories* (London: Routledge, 1991), pp. 311-22 & 324-40.

[16] Ahmed, p. 426.

are dramaturgically performed onstage. What I want to argue here, then, is that normative theatrical forms of narrative realism enable fixity of identity whereby, in the drive for cathartic resolution and satisfactory endings, gay masculinities fall onto either side of Warner's 'good gays/bad queers' binary,[17] which sees 'good gays' rewarded for assimilation into normativity while 'bad queers' are punished, sometimes with AIDS, and always with exclusion from the mainstream. A fragmented, ever-evolving and, crucially, never resolved dramaturgy, on the other hand, situates the spectator within a wide gamut of still-forming, non-hierarchal subjectivities and thus lends itself to the realities of gay masculine subjectivities as they are moved and shaped by – and rail against – heteronormative culture.

Queering Dramaturgy, Queering Homonormativity

In the main, and as *Queen and Peacock* illustrates, traditional Irish narrative drama and realist dramaturgy have not served queer masculinities well. Even contemporary queer realism such as Mark O'Halloran's *Trade* (2011) – a duologue performed in a shabby, by-the-hour boarding house, in which a working-class, married man has a painful, emotionally-charged encounter with a teenage male sex-worker – needs to move into the realm of hyperrealism by becoming site-specific in order to relate its message of interlinked working-class queer-shame and underground sexual economics.[18] Discussing the problems inherent in staging the rich complexities and myriad experiences, both political and everyday, of gay masculinities in contemporary theatre, Alyson Campbell calls for a queer approach to dramaturgy. 'A queer dramaturgy', Campbell argues, 'would be one likely to undermine an identity politics by placing on stage a more fragmented, partial, elliptical structure, with figures who are less "characters" than glimpses of subjectivities in formation.'[19] Yet, up until quite recently, this exploratory, fragmented dramaturgy has been absent from any examination of queerness in Irish theatre.

Campbell's notion of gay masculine 'subjectivities in formation' offers powerful potential for theatrically deconstructing and re-signifying not only homophobic shaming, but especially homonormative shame projected by 'good gays' onto 'bad queers' who do not fall in line with neoliberal commodification of gay identity. Campbell's vision of a queer dramaturgy goes beyond calling gay identity politics and subject formation into question; she also argues for a reimagining of theatrical form, narrative, and structure. Her 'more fragmented, partial, elliptical structure' demands an 'aesthetic regeneration', a 'fast and fluid' theatrical form, 'a certain dramaturgical attitude that resists the

---

[17] Michael Warner, *The Trouble With Normal: Sex, Politics and the Ethics of Queer Life* (Cambridge: Harvard University Press, 1999), p. 114.

[18] Mark O'Halloran, 'Trade' in Thomas Conway, ed., *The Oberon Anthology of Contemporary Irish Plays: This is Just This, It Isn't Real,* It's Money (London: Oberon Books, 2012), pp. 47-81.

[19] Alyson Campbell, 'Translating 'Gaytown: The Collision of Global and Local in Bringing Australian Queer Play *Bison* to Belfast,' *Australasian Drama Studies*, 59 (2011), pp. 141-55, p. 143.

normative dramaturgical frameworks of mainstream (realist) theatre', therefore challenging 'the hegemonic, often binarised, discourses of mainstream ideology and power'.[20] What I want to argue here, then, is that a queering of form, narrative, structure, and the ways we understand traditional characters and characterization, signals the best way forward for theatre that concerns itself with the vicissitudes of queer Irish masculinities. Because realist drama is so identified with socio-normativity, when traditional form and narrative structure are abandoned in favour of a queer dramaturgy then queerness can move towards becoming an intrinsically Irish identity, rather than a set of legislative problems, such as gay marriage or adoption, that are posed as challenges to Irishness. These queer masculinities, by virtue of the radically invigorated aesthetic in which they perform, expose the socio-political and theatrical foundations of regulatory regimes of (homo)normative sexuality, and the ways in which such regimes discursively invent 'bad queers' as social misfits while casting 'good gays' as exemplars of consumership. Or, to put it another way; the queerer the form, the queerer the possibilities for masculine identities.

Thankfully, Irish theatre in the early twenty-first-century quivers with the potential of this queer dramaturgy, as spectators bear witness to a plethora of new performances devised or written by a small cohort of ground-breaking theatre companies and collectives.[21] Of course, these companies are in no small debt to the theatre of Frank McGuinness whose work, since the mid-1980s, has been reconciling queerness and Irish masculinities by utilizing, as David Cregan argues, a dramaturgical 'epistemology [that] is most certainly queer', thus making him the 'first Irish dramatist to rescue the homosexual from the assigned status of object to the self-defining position of subject'.[22] Chronologically parallel to McGuinness, gay theatre company Muted Cupid (a name-change from The Wilde Theatre Workshop) was active in Dublin from 1989 until 1999; yet their dramaturgy could not be called queer, veering more towards realism and drag-cabaret with internationally renowned, iconic gay shows such as *Torch Song Trilogy* staged in 1994. Wet Paint Arts' musical play *Tangles* (1990), which used an 'audience interruption' technique based on the theories of Augusto Boal whereby the spectator could intervene into scenes of homophobic bullying onstage, was a nascent example of this queer dramaturgy. Yet, despite plans to tour community venues where their anti-shaming message would have strong impact, Wet Paint's funding was withdrawn and *Tangles*

[20] Campbell, p. 145, p. 143.

[21] That these performances examine lesbian, bisexual, and transgender subjectivities as much as they interrogate gay male subjectivities is laudable, and it is hoped that future studies by myself or others will interrogate work by queer women practitioners such as Veronica Dyas' *In My Bed*, 2012, and Sonia Kelly's *A Wheelchair on my Face*, 2011. In fact, the book being edited by Miriam Haughton and Mária Kurdi and hopefully appearing at the end of this year, titled Radical Contemporary Theatre Practices by Women in Ireland (to be published with Carysfort Press) has papers in it about queer women performers including Dyas.

[22] David Cregan, 'Coming Out: Frank McGuinness's Dramaturgy and Queer Resistance', *Irish University Review*, 40:1 (2010), pp. 46-58, p. 58, p. 46.

remained confined to a city-centre theatre.[23] Hence, after *Tangles* closed in 1993, queer dramaturgy lay dormant until companies like THISISPOPBABY, TheatreofplucK, PettyCash, and THEATRE Machine took up the mantle in the mid-2000s. Finding a home primarily in radical performance festivals like Dublin Fringe, Queer Notions, OUTBURST Queer Arts, and the Dublin Gay Theatre Festival,[24] (and, in the last three years, spilling into the Dublin International Theatre Festival), these companies showcase the work of queer producers, practitioners, writers, and performers such as Neil Watkins, Shane Byrne, Mark O'Halloran, Phillip McMahon, Panti Bliss, and Oisín McKenna. These festivals and the performers they host create, as Fintan Walsh puts it, 'a safe but also clearly defined space for conceptions of queer identity to develop and express itself, while simultaneously working to contest narrow prescriptions of national identity and cultural performance.'[25]

Labile not only in form and structure, but also in venue-choice, queer dramaturgy signals a shift away from conventional theatre auditoria and seating arrangements. Sometimes, queer theatre in Ireland happens in theatre lobbies rather than in the theatre itself, at nightclubs, on bar-counters in gay pubs, in abandoned business premises, in alternative cafés, and on the streets. It can be impromptu, like when the opening night of Neil Watkins' monologue *The Year of Magical Wanking* (2010) had to be stopped about twenty minutes into the performance due to a power-outage in the Temple Bar area of Dublin.[26] Watkins, not to be deterred, stuck a beer-keg into a snow-drift on the wintry street outside and, jumping up on the keg, performed a fifteen-minute medley of scenes and songs from the show and his other work. Queer dramaturgy, when it does happen in traditional theatre spaces, has veered towards more leftist, radical, or community venues such as Dublin's New Theatre and Project Arts Centre, Ballymun's Axis, or Belfast's MAC.

That the choice of such venues is usually driven by economic concerns resonates with the most vital function of a queer dramaturgy: its ability to call into question, for both spectator and critic, the neoliberal commodification of gay male identities that have become increasingly market-driven since decriminalization in 1993. Commercialized gay identity, best promulgated by handholding gay men through a tollbooth economy that dictates how they purchase and so perform their gayness, is therefore countered by queer politics

---

[23] For a full history of *Tangles* including a discussion of the funding withdrawal, see its director David Grant's essay 'Tangles: Addressing an Unusual Audience' in Éibhear Walsh, ed., *Sex, Nation and Dissent in Irish Writing* (Cork: Cork University Press, 1997), pp. 235-51.

[24] In 2010 the organizational committee of the Dublin Gay Theatre Festival announced that, for reasons of commercial sponsorship, the committee had bifurcated and henceforth there would be a second festival, the Absolut Gay Theatre Festival. See Brian Merriman, *Wilde Stages in Dublin: A Decade of Gay Theatre* (Dublin: International Gay Theatre Festival Ltd, 2013), pp. 171-79.

[25] Fintan Walsh, 'Shirley Temple Bar at the Abbey: Irish Theatre, Queer Performance and the Politics of Disidentification', *Irish Theatre International*, 1.1 (2008), pp. 53-72, pp. 57-58.

[26] Neil Watkins, 'The Year of Magical Wanking' in Conroy, ed., *Oberon Anthology*, pp. 291-323.

and dramaturgies that seek to dismantle such regimes by fostering welfare-orientated collectives where masculine identities are not bought and sold, but explored and discovered through kinship and corporeal and sexual freedom. Queer dramaturgy undermines commodified gay-male perfection, and pokes holes in the populist narrative of happy, apolitical 'A-gays' with lucrative careers that provide ample leisure time in which to pursue costly activities: a market-driven reification that fundamentally, as Sarah Schulman asserts, 'replaces most people's experiences with the perceptions of the privileged and calls that reality.'[27] Instead, through Campbell's 'complex, non-linear dramaturgy that [...] shares a queer resistance to fixing identity', we encounter self-doubting, still-forming, sometimes unhappy, queer masculinities, and so move towards a fuller understanding of the non-mainstream gay men who face the challenges of unemployment and precarious existence, of HIV and its incumbent stigma, of disability, or of racial discrimination, and are yet politically involved and often full of rage at the status-quo.

Queer Dramaturgy in Performance

For the spectator, queer dramaturgy in performance is experiential, floating through, above, and around both psychic and sensory affects. As well as engaging spectators in their traditional tasks of listening to spoken dialogue while watching bodies enact a story, queer dramaturgy simultaneously, often very determinedly, mobilizes sonic and lighting landscapes, sometimes even involving smell and touch. Scenography and set-pieces, when they exist, are mobile, multi-functional, symbolic: a steel rectangle on wheels is one moment a doorway to exit or enter, the next a picture-frame with a living subject, the next a coffin in which a body lies dead, but might yet come back to life. Words spoken by actors can move a story along, or they could be meta-commentary, an outsider's point of view offering narrative possibilities or changing the scene. While there are still traditional antagonists and protagonists, characterization is non-hierarchal, characters meld in and out of each other, an actor is one minute a primary protagonist, the next an anonymous voice in a crowd. Fixed ideas of masculinity, manhood, and male sexuality are therefore called into question, become pluralized, often negated, as received knowledge and assumptions about Irish men and masculinities, rooted in hetero- and homonormativity, are disrupted. Yet, this disruption often remains just that, a fragmentation of male sexual identity that offers no reassembling, no fixed solutions, but rather leaves spectators to formulate their own answers about Irish masculine sexualities and subjectivities.

Two recent shows, *Bison* (2009) and *The Trouble with Harry* (2013), produced by Belfast-based TheatreofplucK, are primary exemplars of Irish queer dramaturgy.[28] Both are written by Australian-born playwright Lachlan

---

[27] Sarah Schulman, *The Gentrification of the Mind: Witness to a Lost Imagination* (Berkeley: University of California Press, 2012), p. 161.

[28] Lachlan Philpott, 'Bison' in *Bison & Colder* (Sydney: Playlab Press, 2010), pp. 13-68. Unpublished script of *The Trouble with Harry* kindly provided by Lachlan Philpott.

Philpott and were originally set in Sydney, which would seem initially to pose problems to the Irishness of the pieces. However, a geopolitical dramaturgical translation, facilitated by a collaborative workshop approach that prioritizes input from writer, actors, director, scenography and sound designers, and the stage crew who must bring this queer dramaturgy into material reality on a tiny budget, enabled *Bison* and *Harry*'s transposition into an Irish dramatic idiom.

Trouble with Harry raises questions about not only the fixity of socially constructed manhood and patriarchal sexuality, but also examines, through a performance of female masculinity, the lived realities of a subject who, unlike the majority of biological males that perform manhood without realizing it, must undertake painful, self-taught, and ultimately fatal lessons about the ways in which sanctioned male identity and sexuality are formed and performed in everyday life. The play explores the history of 'female husband' Eugenie Falleni (1875-1938), an Italian-born immigrant to Australia who lived most of her life as Harry Crawford, and was convicted for the murder of her 'wife', Annie Birkett, in Sydney in 1920. *Harry* is set in 1917, the final year of Annie and Harry's marriage, and chronicles Annie's discovery of Harry's biological femaleness, and the fear of public disclosure that propelled him to murder her. The geopolitical translation into a Belfast schema worked, as was made clear in the post-show audience discussion, through accent and scenographic ambiguity. The cast all had strong Northern Irish accents that some spectators decoded as being an Irish family recently emigrated to Sydney; for some they had just returned back to Belfast from Australia; for others Sydney never entered their schema and the play was set in Belfast; for others the play was based in a generic industrial city where locale made no difference and was never a thinking-point during viewing.[29]

Conveying a sense of masculinity entrapped not just in the wrong body but also in poverty, the scenography – comprised mainly of steel frames of varying rectangle shapes and sizes on castor-wheels that the cast moved seamlessly around the playing-area – situates the spectator in the industrial dystopia of an early-twentieth-century cityscape, and simultaneously in Crawford's mind. Creating a sharp, jarring juxtaposition to the surreal, ever moving steel-frames, Harry (played by a woman), Annie, and their children, Josephine and Harry Junior (both from previous marriages when Harry lived as a woman), wear historically accurate costumes and enact their story in a realistic playing style. Two non- or anti-characters dressed in modern-day costume, Man and Woman, stand outside of the action, slinking around the stage, making comment, guiding spectators through the story, delivering the lines of minor characters such as neighbours or policemen, and, to capture the scandal that engulfed Falleni, passing scornful judgement.

Yet, Man and Woman's dramaturgical function goes beyond story-narration and scene setting; they incite the spectator to doubt the fixity of official

---

[29] Post-show discussion, *The Trouble With Harry*, at the Mac, Belfast, 23 November 2013; documented in TheatreofplucK archives at Outburst Queer Arts Festival offices, 8-22 Hill Street, Belfast, BT1 2LA.

histories, while simultaneously raising questions about from whose point of view such histories are told. At several crucial plot points they present narrative alternatives: 'what if she'd done this instead?' or 'what if he'd gone there instead?'

> WOMAN: What does she say to him? Does she say/
> JOSEPHINE: I'm sure he just cut himself. It'll heal.
> MAN: Is it that? Is that what she says? Or does she say/
> JOSEPHINE: You were probably half asleep and dreaming [...]
> WOMAN: Or is it?
> JOSEPHINE: I need to tell you something Harry.
> HARRY: What?
> MAN: There? She's going to tell him there?
> WOMAN: There. Yes.
> MAN: What's she going to tell him? What words will she say?[30]

Oscillating the spectator thus between the sexual topographies of 2013 and 1917, a time in history when pathologizing discourses of homosexuality were gaining medical, psychological, and cultural currency, *Harry*'s queer dramaturgy throws current and historical paradigms of socially sanctioned manhood into disarray, disrupting notions of sexual essentialism and labelling, as well as foregrounding the ways in which queer masculine sexualities are still pathologized today. Phallocentric taxonomies such as 'lesbian', 'homosexual', 'passive', 'active', 'penetrator', and 'intercourse' are destabilized. This is most prescient during the scene when Josephine, Harry's daughter from his previous female existence who has now come back into his life, relates how she found 'the thing, the snake'[31] – in reality a home-made dildo that enabled Annie and Harry's patriarchal sex, which, as a later scene conveys through narration and vocal utterance, was frequent and pleasurable. And yet, upon his disclosure, Annie claims ignorance of Harry's biological femaleness, further complicating notions of knowing and not knowing, of complicity and duplicity, of penetrator and penetrated. Overall, what *Harry*'s queer dramaturgy drives home with an unexpected finality is that, both socially and theatrically, we can never fully understand nor categorize masculine sexualities, that cultural assumptions about maleness, manhood, and how men have sex are as varied and complicated as the free-form, fragmented theatre event happening before our eyes.

Parallel to *Bison* and *Trouble with Harry*, other queer dramaturgies are beginning to permeate the Irish theatre scene, with shows usually starting in Belfast or Dublin, and then touring the country and abroad. THISISPOPBABY are the most polemic and prolific company in this regard. Their camp musical fantasia *Alice in Funderland*, which started life as a workshop reading in 2010, received a main-stage production as the Abbey Theatre's summer show of 2012. *Elevator* (2012), written and directed by company founder Phillip McMahon, mobilized a queer dramaturgy – including carnivalesque sequences with

30 Lachlan Philpott, *The Trouble with Harry*, 54-55.
31 Ibid., p. 32.

characters donning horse-heads to perform scenes of bacchanalian excess – thus questioning received notions of wealth, privilege, and masculine bisexuality at a time when the country is being fed a political narrative of conservative austerity.[32] THISISPOPBABY have also queered theatrical space with a series of 'Performance. Art. Club' events, called *Werk*, which take place in the lobby of the Abbey Theatre's studio space, The Peacock. A mish-mash of monologues, poetry slam, solo singers, bands, performance art, and idiosyncratic personalities from the Dublin alternative scene who mingle with spectators, just being queer, the glue that binds *Werk*'s sporadic occurrences is Neil Watkins' role as MC. In all of his performances as *Werk*'s MC, apart from one, Watkins costumed himself as a queered-up version of the traditional Irish newscaster or television presenter. RTÉ, the state broadcaster, has its own particular history of these generic male presenters, each one like a carbon copy of his previous incarnation. Watkins' queer riffs on this urbane, intrinsically Irish hetero-masculinity is made all the more ironic in that his paternal uncle is Gay Byrne who was the first and most famous of this lineage of television personalities.

Queering the Monologue

In terms of challenging both homophobic and homonormative shaming, one of the most significant inroads queer dramaturgies have made is into the monologue. Monodrama is now entrenched in Irish theatrical culture as a particularly masculinist form. Irish spectators have born witness to two decades of monologues about hetero-masculinity in crisis, in which, as Brian Singleton asserts, 'socially subordinated male individuals [...] are performing their own abjection in a society in which they have lost their place.'[33] There has been, however, a queer appropriation of the male monologue, an assertive disavowal of what Eamonn Jordan identifies as 'the masculinity gone astray' model so prominent in previous laddish monodramas.[34] By disrupting spectators' expectations of the form, and making queer the interlocutors' traditional role of hetero-masculine story-teller, this queering goes beyond merely challenging hegemonic patriarchy.

In his 2005 monologue *A Cure for Homosexuality*, first performed as part of the Dublin Gay Theatre Festival, Neil Watkins disrupts expectations of a ninety-minute, continual, realist story delivered by a hetero-loser, on several levels.[35] First, the monologue was performed not in a theatre but in Dublin's Centre Stage café, a popular gay venue. However, in a queer twist on setting and scenography, Watkins announced that 'the play is set in a café' where 'the

---

32 Unpublished scripts of *Alice in Funderland* and *Elevator* kindly provided by Phillip McMahon.

33 Brian Singleton, *Masculinities and the Contemporary Irish Theatre* (Basingstoke: Palgrave Macmillan, 2011), p. 71.

34 Eamonn Jordan, *Dissident Dramaturgies: Contemporary Irish Theatre* (Dublin: Irish Academic Press, 2010), p. 222.

35 Neil Watkins, 'A Cure For Homosexuality' in Walsh, ed., *Queer Notions*, pp. 111-35.

audience is its customers',[36] thereby creating not only a *mise en abyme* (picture-within-a-picture) of a never-ending performative loop of queer male sexuality, but also giving free reign to audience members to make what they would of their dual roles as café customers and theatre spectators. During the performance spectators ate, drank, moved about, summoned waiters, called out to Watkins and passed comment, while still observing the unwritten rules of spectatorship by not causing undue disturbance to the show. This in turn enabled Watkins to integrate these customer/spectator activities into his performance as they happened.

Second, the monologue is divided into four acts rather than the standard continuous piece. As well as disrupting expectations of form and length, this enables a queer semiotics whereby for each act Watkins' character, Paddy Doyle, donned a statement-costume that played on popular stereotypes of gay masculinity. In Act I Paddy is dressed in 'a leather Nazi uniform',[37] the Nazi theme making dangerous the by-now sanitized iconicity of the gay Leatherman. Act II sees him 'dressed like an all-American boy-next-door', a comment on the heteronormativity and HIV-shaming which the show critiques. For Act III he makes an affectionate nod to queer theatre history, appearing 'in full glamour drag' and opens the act by singing 'a seductive show tune that enthuses and titillates'. And for Act IV 'Paddy wears an outrageously camp outfit', thus bucking the homonormative valorization of 'straight acting' gays.[38]

The third and most crucial queering element of Watkins' monologue lies in the structure and content of Paddy's spoken narrative. Paddy's tale starts in the S&M clubs of Berlin where he contracts HIV when a bondage scenario with his Leather Master becomes non-consensual. Act II sees Paddy in evangelical America, now a born-again Christian in 'The Church of Christ and the Burning Bush' – chief minister, George 'Dubya' Bush.[39] Settling into a decade of heteronormative, bible-belt Republicanism, he has, in a critique of the controversial Christian movement, 'prayed away the gay'. In Act III, however, Paddy, in his glamour-drag, reveals that 'my wife's clothes did prove too much of a temptation for me'.[40] When his church realize not only that his queerness remains uncured, but also that he is HIV-positive, they imprison him in a concentration camp where he falls in love with Angel, the male commandant. Angel forces Paddy into gender-reassignment surgery to socially normalize their love, which mysteriously cures Paddy's HIV. Yet, by Act IV, Paddy is back in Dublin, very definitely male, very definitely gay, and very definitely HIV-positive. Paddy therefore realizes that the cure for homosexuality, according to fundamentalist right-wing America, is, in fact, AIDS. AIDS will rid the world of queerness if, as various governments have demonstrated, it is ignored and denied vital research funding.

[36] Ibid., 111.
[37] Ibid.
[38] Ibid., pp. 124, 129.
[39] Ibid., p. 120.
[40] Ibid., p. 124.

In this monologue Watkins transcends the boundaries between the fictional Paddy and the live performer. Conor McPherson's realist narratives of hard men in tough trouble stand in stark contrast to Paddy's wild, obviously fictional story and fantastical scenarios. The crazy stories function as a separating device between character and actor. However, despite this separation, certain aspects of Watkins' performance such as spectator interaction, references to Dublin locations, a localized camp-vernacular – his rootedness in Dublin gay culture – engender a slippage between Paddy-as-character and Watkins-as-performer. This slippage creates audience identification and empathy, thus drawing the spectator into both their own and mainstream society's complicity in homophobic, HIV, and homonormative shaming in much more explicit ways than, for example, the happy rush towards homonormativity that Paul in *Queen and Peacock* undertakes.

Other queer monologists play with the form. Drag artiste Panti Bliss, in a trilogy of monologues, *In These Shoes* (2007), *A Woman in Progress* (2009), and *All Dolled Up: Restitched* (2013),[41] recounts a life lived in queer space and time while simultaneously sounding a rallying cry against politically apathetic gay men and the commodification of gay identities. Most polemically, Panti used the monologue to highlight issues of homophobia in Ireland. Invited onto the Abbey stage to deliver the 'Noble Call' – a guest monologue at the end of every performance of James Plunkett's *The Risen People* in which prominent figures in Irish life speak on matters of social importance – Panti delivered a rousing speech during a time when national media outlets were permitting a Catholic lobby group to lay down the terms by which homophobia can be understood and talked about. 'In a spectacular, neat Orwellian twist', Panti told the world, 'gay people in Ireland are no longer the victims of homophobia. Now it seems homophobes are the victims of homophobia.'[42] The video of Panti's speech had, within three days, been seen and commented upon by media outlets worldwide, with messages of support from celebrities such as Madonna, Stephen Fry, and Dame Edna Average, and has been used to open and frame several debates on homophobia both nationally and internationally.

Shane Byrne's monologue *Hungry/Tender* (2012) shifts the concerns of the young male monologist from the masculine public world into the realm of the corporeal.[43] Byrne highlights the constructedness of hegemonic patriarchy as it shifts on its own contingencies by interrogating the contradictions inherent in a culture that expects men to perform a rugged, hard-bodied masculinity while conversely engaging in traditionally feminine behaviours and thought patterns regarding body image and cosmetic appearance. Byrne's monologist has an eating disorder and, stemming from that, issues of body image and self-esteem, traditionally crises associated with women and femininity. 'I knew I couldn't be

---

[41] *All Dolled Up: Restitched* is a re-working of Panti's previous monologue from 2007, *All Dolled Up*. Grateful thanks to Phillip McMahon who provided scripts of all three shows over the years.

[42] Panti Bliss, 'The Noble Call' performed at The Abbey Theatre, Dublin, 1 February 2014.

[43] Unpublished script of *Hungry/Tender* kindly provided by Shane Byrne.

the only guy who felt this way', Byrne says about why he wrote the monologue, 'I think it's time we looked at this new male body culture and started to give men a break.'[44] Critiqued by reviewers as being 'self-indulgent' and 'an onstage therapy session',[45] Byrne nonetheless gives voice to a new generation of young men who want to question a body-conscious advertising and media culture that promulgates the well-toned, tanned male body as the only culturally acceptable paradigm of physical maleness.

Like Watkins, Byrne breaks with conventions of narrative storytelling. There are long silences during the performance while he cooks his beloved yet forbidden toasted cheese sandwiches with which to secretly feed his counter-homonormative body. These drawn-out silences are awkward for the spectator, and go towards casting the discomfort of queer bodies in normative culture back out into the audience. In a further act of defiance against homonormative shaming, Byrne leaves the stage empty for what feels like an overly long time. He reappears wearing glamour underwear, and proceeds to draw cosmetic surgery lines all over his body with a red marker, highlighting for the spectator the exact parts of his body about which he refuses to feel shame, while simultaneously making spectators aware of their own complicity in a culture of bodily shaming.

Billing himself as a 'spoken word artist' rather than an actor, in his monologue *Grindr: A Love Story*, Oisín McKenna performs the disjuncture between lived male bodies and the virtual perfection of homonormativity as it is constructed online on gay hook-up websites such as *Gaydar, Manhunt,* and *Grindr*.[46] McKenna articulates the peer surveillance of online masculine construction, reiterating Mowlabocus' point that Internet sexual spaces facilitate a 'pornification' of gay male lives. 'In the acts of browsing, searching and categorizing that occur in this web space', Mowlabocus argues, gay masculinities 'move beyond the representational' into a virtual imaginary, where 'sexual identity is produced, negotiated, and maintained'.[47] Online peer-surveillance becomes self-surveillance, which, as McKenna makes clear, then morphs into self-shaming. McKenna's performance intervenes into this cycle, both within himself and in regimes of the commodified homonormal.

Disavowing the exclusionary protest of McPherson's disenfranchised men who seek assimilation into the patriarchal order, monologists like Watkins, Byrne, and McKenna colonize the hetero-masculinist storyteller role, thus queering the Irish tradition of the Seanchaí. That both Byrne and McKenna have come up under the talent-nurturing auspices of THEATRE Club, while Watkins' *The Year of Magical Wanking* has been produced and internationally toured by THISISPOPBABY, indicates a nascent yet growing theatrical zeitgeist of queer male monologists who wish to expose not just the narrow limitations

44 Author interview with Shane Byrne, March 2013.

45 Sara Keating, 'Review: Hungry/Tender', *Irish Times*, 14 September 2012.

46 Unpublished script of *Grindr: A Love Story* kindly provided by Oisín McKenna.

47 Mowlabocus, p. 63.

of commodified, sanitized gay masculinity, but also the social processes and structures of gay shaming, both homophobic and homonormative.

Conclusions

Essentially, queer dramaturgies foreground the correlations between paradigmatic shifts in capitalism and discursively constructed gay male identities in Ireland since the early-1990s. Just as capitalism is no longer managed by governments, but driven by what economists call 'self-regulating markets',[48] so too have gay men shifted from being politically-controlled and aware citizens into market-driven tropes of identity. Irish political theorist Sean Phelan argues that neoliberalism, as it moves through Irish politics and culture, takes on two forms: 'transparent' or 'euphemistic'.[49] Transparent neoliberalism is easily identified, and makes no claims to be anything other than a championing of big business and free markets above the needs of the citizenry. Euphemistic neoliberalism, on the other hand, hides itself in 'media-savvy' discourses of 'pragmatism' and 'consensus', and 'avoids over identification with the market', instead mobilizing signifiers such as 'modern' and 'non-ideological' – and glosses its machinations in a sheen of misaligned consumer 'choice'.[50] Following Phelan, I conclude here, then, that gay masculinities performing within queer dramaturgical strategies shift neoliberal political and cultural practices out of the realm of the euphemistic, and expose them to the spectator by making them transparent.

In the final analysis, queer dramaturgies can propel Irish theatre into a performative discourse whereby gay masculinities – through explorations of queer subjectivities in formation, and by resisting neoliberal socio-political and cultural forces that seek to mould gay lives and living into commodified homonormativity – are afforded the theatrical freedom to claim their own understandings of Irishness and thus be Irishmen. When gay men perform alternative, radical forms of queer masculinities other than a market-driven version of homogenous Western gayness, then such performances can begin to interrogate how a queer culture sees itself, rather than how it is reified and cast into homonormativity by a neoliberal economy. And, how a queer culture sees and understands itself is, I would argue, far more crucial than how neoliberal markets imagine it.

CORMAC O'BRIEN has recently completed his PhD on Masculinities in Contemporary Irish Theatre at the School of English, Drama, and Film at University College Dublin, where he teaches part-time. Cormac's research interests lie in contemporary Irish and British theatre, queer theatre and queer theatre histories, and gender and sexuality in performance. Stemming from his

---

48 David Harvey, *A Brief History of Neoliberalism* (Oxford: Oxford UP, 2005), p.184-85.

49 Sean Phelan, 'Irish Neoliberalism, Media, and the Politics of Discourse', in Debbie Ging, Michael Cronin, & Peadar Kirby, eds., *Transforming Ireland: Challenges, Critiques, Resources*, p. 73-78, p. 75.

50 Phelan, 'Irish Neoliberalism', p. 75.

PhD research, Cormac is developing new research into biopolitics in theatre, particularly the ways in which HIV and AIDS – and the bodies they occupy – are represented in performance. Cormac has published several essays and book chapters in edited collections and journals such as *Irish University Review*, *Theatre Research International*, and *The Hungarian Journal of English and American Studies*. Cormac gratefully acknowledges the support of the Irish Research Council, and the Graduate Research and Education Programme in Gender, Identity, and Culture at UCD.

Hungry Tender (2012) by Shane Byrne for TheatreCLUB. Performer: Shane Byrne. Image by kind permission of Fiona Morgan.

The Trouble with Harry (2013) by Lachlan Philpott for TheatreofplucK. Performers: Stephanie Weyman, Gordon Mahn, Michelle Wiggins, Matthew Mitchell, Roisin Gallagher. Image by kind permission of Simon Crawford.

'Perform, or else!'

NEIL WATKINS

'Tell your story.' They were the words that came in the middle of the night. I had wanted to die. Depression ran the show for me. And some weird spiritual event bled into my fragile reality. Jesus appeared to me in my bedroom and asked me if I still wanted to die. Yeah Jesus..., you read it right. I thought of my family who lived up the road. 'No, I said.' 'I want to stay.' And Jesus said: 'Then tell your story.'

Obviously I'm mad. I'll allow you the space to consider that as a justification for my unusual experience. Or it is just your thinking. I'm okay with you thinking that I'm mad. But my heartfelt opinion is that my work has value. I like it. I stand by it.

Frustrated by the unequal distribution of arts wealth on stages of all shapes and sizes and a blatant blind lack of cop-on from artists' work, and crippled by my own insatiable inner critic, it was just becoming impossible to enjoy anything. I guess I've been a nightmare to go to the theatre with. An ex of mine gave up accompanying me. The stain of being a hyper-critical drama student doesn't fade easily. I needed to heal the demon in me.

Years of chronic pain and an exciteable ego in bloom obliterated my chances of following the conventional path. My task became making work that catered to my taste and my needs. Perform or die. Tell my story or suffer in silence while others went ahead whether I liked it or not.

A terrifying medical condition bubbled beneath the pain, the resentment and the tortured artist persona. And oh I had so much to draw on. Eventually I exposed myself through iambic pentametre's thin veil as I waxed lyrical about my elaborate masturbation strategy to fill the void in my solo slice of indulgence, *The Year of Magical Wanking*. Enabled by the precision of THISISPOPBABY's production, I worked out many demons. The play's ability to return to a stage somewhere time and again ensured one vital thing: my staying alive.

At first, vanity was the carrot dangling in front of me. I transformed from little donkey to black swan. Magically a well paid commercial for a household name came my way so I could fund my health regime. I invested in bikram yoga and a personal trainer and I was pretty cut in time for the Dublin Fringe. But who cares about appearances. Fitness is about how you feel. And of course, who you get to lay with. Sorry that was my ego ... it's about how you feel.

The need for validation was certainly a reason to stand up before a multitude of strangers and bear all. Growing up in the MTV generation dreams of fame tickled my fancy. As did riches. But I'm an innocent victim of media culture. I was sold a lie.

The aftermath of *The Year of Magical Wanking* has been the best of times/worst of times descent into Wonderland. I've had headaches that make it impossible for me to concentrate. I have to do yoga, shamanic healing and therapy to get through the day. Drink and drugs are just not on the cards for me. Its been a long time coming. My ego has to die.

I was invited to the Abbey to see *Twelfth Night* by William Shakespeare. Let me say that I've had some magical experiences at The Abbey. Years ago as a teenager, I saw my first Shakepearean play, *The Comedy of Errors*, directed by one of my long time mentors Gerard Stembridge. I remember not fully understanding the language of Shakespeare but the production and the feeling from it penetrated my being.

On another occasion I was in a tricky place. I was making a piece for the Fringe called *The Dark Room*. This would be the first time to write about my HIV diagnosis and my experience of being molested as a child. Frightened by what I was about to do I needed some sort of angel to appear. And one week before my show opened I sat down in the Abbey to watch *An Ideal Husband*. Soon the seat next to me filled up with one of my queer idols. He was Justin Bond, whose Kiki And Herb Concert at Carnegie Hall was my bible. We hung out for the entire night and got drunk and sang songs at a lock-in in Kenny's Bar in Kilmainham. It was magical.

I don't like opening nights. That pressure. I dread the hugs that I seem to be forced to give when usually I walk away feeling empty about the work. It astounds me in this day and age when TV shows like *Breaking Bad* and *True Detective* are the benchmark for captivating people's hearts, that a complete lack of awareness of accessiblity for the audience is overlooked by many of today's art makers.

A trip to the theatre too often is an ordeal for me. And the only way I can do anything about it is to not bitch about it, but get up off my arse and make the kind of work I would like to see. The ego on display sometimes assures me that we are lost in a sad state of affairs. What seems to be more important than a connection with the audience is a self conscious effort to tick the boxes, to put bums on seats, to pepper the holes with gadgets and gizmos. And perhaps most wasteful of all, to throw large sums of cash at design that doesn't serve anything. We are drowning.

The reviews roll in and Facebook fills up with back slapping. God knows we all try whatever we can to get the crowd in. Next year there will be awards. Like the Oscars, which once I loved but now like most grown ups see them for what they are. Art, art, art, is suffering because of self consciousness, fear and ego. And the standard from the Irish Institutions is sending out the wrong message to the masses. Work is too often soulless. As long as the emperor is wearing his new clothes there'll be plenty of lick arses to keep him where he loves to be.

And it's all innocent. Everyone is doing their best. Everyone clings on to the status and the politics and the next round of funding. We are all doing our best. But we deserve more from Art. So I'm not going to wait for the big boys to deliver to me the thing I need. What I need is to do it myself. I need to change the channel. I need to be nice about it. I gather people around me who will not tell me that my clothes are beautiful when in fact I'm not wearing any.

I wish all the funding in the arts was cut. And that the board of this and the board of that would disappear. And then we'll see who connects with the audience. Perhaps from that place a product that an audience genuinely needs can emerge... something to make you laugh, to make you cry, to make you feel. God rest Shakespeare and Wilde and all the greats. I just wish they'd be left to rest in peace, at least until somebody with big enough balls and brains tackles their artistic expression with integrity. And I wish that for now, the artists who are alive today and who know from first hand experience what it is to live in this world of now are connected with producers savvy and grounded enough to recognize their vitality. We the audience of today need the art of today.

But whatever, different strokes for different folks. We are all doing our best. I'm happy as long as I get to do my own thing. I'm happy as long as I demonstrate my own vision and standard. Peace.

NEIL WATKINS lives in Dublin. Following a comprehensive stint at Dublin Youth Theatre, he went on to study acting at Drama Centre London. As writer, his plays include *A Cure for Homosexuality*, *Love in the time of Affluence*, *The Dark Room*, *Dublin City Counselling*, *The Year of Magical Wanking* and *Dinner and A Show*. He is a regular feature writer for Cult Magazine and RTÉ Radio's Arena. With music collaborator and friend TIM O'DONOVAN he is one half of pop duo Buffalo Woman. Neil has collaborated with THISISPOPBABY and THEATREclub and has toured internationally with SEAN MILLAR's and BrokenTalkers Silver Stars. With collaborator and friend James O Driscoll he has directed *Tear it Down* (Project) and *Yeah Partner* (Smock Alley). The pair are developing a new play for Dublin Fringe 2014. Neil works part-time and eats full-time at the Fumbally Cafe, does the occasional commercial or voice over and also bits and pieces of TV and film.

Book Reviews

Matthew Yde, *Bernard Shaw and Totalitarianism: Longing for Utopia* (Basingstoke: Palgrave Macmillan, 2013), 247 pp., €16.99 (paperback) ISBN 978-1-137-30192

Reviewed by Audrey McNamara

In *Bernard Shaw and Totalitarianism: Longing for Utopia,* author Matthew Yde argues for Bernard Shaw's engagement with a utopian vision for society. He maintains that 'Shaw desperately needed to restore order through imagining utopian perfection' (2-3). This utopian vision manifested itself, according to Yde, in an admiration for the emerging totalitarian regimes under Stalin, Hitler, and especially Mussolini in the intervening years between the two world wars. In the introduction to the book Yde is very careful to state that he does not expect nor want, what he describes as 'this neglected version' (24) in his study of the work of Shaw to become the dominant version. His intention rather is to make a contribution to a richer and more complete understanding of Shaw and his writings. There is no doubt that this is certainly a thought-provoking work that should and will incite Shavian scholars to defend and reply to Yde's treatise.

The book examines a selection of Shaw's dramatic and non-dramatic writings spanning the sixty-year period of his writing career beginning with Shaw's book *The Quintessence of Ibsenism* (1891) and ending with his last completed play in 1950, the year of his death, *Farfetched Fables.* Yde explores what he terms as Shaw's exhibition of 'a kind of Manichaean thinking' (19) through a duality of his own by aligning one of Shaw's other major essays of the 1890s, *The Perfect Wagnerite* (1898) with *The Quintessence of Ibsenism* as an investigation into Shaw's treatise on the value of and indeed his perceived need for a utopian society that would eradicate the evils of a capitalist society. Yde maintains that 'Shaw himself needed to break free from the constraints of law, the burden of believing in a transcendent moral code, a code that so wracked his conscience of his youth and that he now believed was a sham' (65). Yde argues for Shaw's engagement with the concept of a 'Creative Evolution', a 'Life Force' which constituted the biological improvement of the human race, the purging of those deemed to be 'unfit' and 'unworthy' to maintain their position in a world that denounced parasitic idleness.

Eight of Shaw's dramatic writings form the basis for Yde's analysis of Shaw's Utopian Self. Although he does allude to several other plays as being equally valuable, he does not investigate them in any great depth. He begins his investigation with *Man and Superman* (1903), *John Bull's Other Island* (1904) and *Major Barbara* (1905) as a trilogy that present Shaw's Utopian dream. Yde maintains that in *Man and Superman* Shaw extends the notion of Creative Evolution when the character of Tanner acknowledges the destructiveness within himself as a necessary trait for the survival of mankind. He continues the argument stating that the writing of *John Bull's Other Island* led Shaw to a dead end that was rectified by the writing of *Major Barbara* in which he transforms Tom Broadbent into the clear visionary character of Andrew Undershaft. These plays, Yde argues, point to Shaw's revolutionary self. In examining *Back to Methuselah* (1918-20), he continues to argue that this play is the product of Shaw's utopian imagination (114), containing a 'picture of the world as Shaw wished to see it and evidently believed the Life Force was leading it' (115). Moving on in the next chapter to Shaw's drama of the 1930's and the period that Yde terms as the 'period of totalitarianism proper' (20), he examines the plays *Geneva* and *The Millionairess* both written in 1936 and *The Simpleton of the Unexpected Isles* (1934), exploring them as Shavian investigations of the notions of government and leadership, by interrogating within the works, fascism, communism, and democracy. The final chapter deals with *Farfetched Fables* (1950) which Yde maintains is a 'sort of reworking of *Back to Methuselah* thereby enforcing the themes of the earlier play' (185) and is 'a species of the Utopian genre' (186). He analyses it in the light of the atrocities of World War II and finds it remarkable that Shaw appears to have overlooked the horrors perpetrated during the war and continues to persist, in his dramatic writings, with the Utopian ideal of the Superman and Creative Evolution. In a balance to the argument of the book, Yde's epilogue deals with and acknowledges to some degree a selection of Shaw's contemporaries who also had an admiration or leaning towards the fascist and communist regimes that were developing through the first half of the twentieth century such as W. B. Yeats, a fellow countryman, Ezra Pound, and T. S Eliot.

Yde's final summary appears to paint Shaw as a supremacist whose vision for the world does not include the nuclear family as part of a stable and prosperous society. However, the overall tone of the book does not convey this as a reality. Time and time again it becomes obvious through the analysis that Bernard Shaw's utopian views were idealistic and reactionary to the political and social climate of the time rather than despotic. There is no question that Shaw admired Mussolini, Lenin, and even Hitler, and it is possible that his own personal views of what society should be like could have clouded his better judgement in regard to how those utopian aims were achieved in the totalitarian regimes of the era. In relation to this Yde actually quotes from an address that Shaw gave to the BBC in 1937, which bears testament to the fact that killing and waste were an unnecessary part of 'putting our house in order'

(195). As Yde points out, Shaw was not isolated in his admiration for the dictators of the era and it can be argued that there is very strong evidence within this book for putting these views into their historical context. History has shown that dictators like Mussolini, Lenin, Hitler, and Stalin have a capacity to stimulate and motivate nations. They offered, what appeared to be, an alternative to the oppressive capitalism. Notwithstanding that the solution they implemented resulted in the worst kind of oppression, the regard for these dictators was not just confined to their own countries. The British Prime Minister of the time, Winston Churchill, professed Mussolini a great and wise man. His admiration for the politician persisted two years after Mussolini aligned himself with Hitler (Patrick Buchanan, *Churchill, Hitler and the Unnecessary War: How Britain Lost an Empire* [New York: Random House, 2008], p. 160). In addition, the then Taoiseach and future President of Ireland, Eamonn de Valera, paid a visit to the German legation to offer condolences on the death of Hitler in 1945. These historical facts demonstrate the power, allure, and control that accompanied the communist and fascist regimes of the day. Historical context is paramount in understanding the political and social thinking of the time and cannot be discounted for a balanced and effective argument.

Bernard Shaw and Totalitarianism: Longing for Utopia is an excellently written and well researched book. Its subject matter is long overdue in the Shavian canon, not least for the fact that it will air the cupboard on Shaw's politics and should galvanize debate on this lesser explored side to Shaw's political thinking. To quote Shaw himself 'If you can't get rid of the skeleton in your closet, you'd best take him out and make him dance' (Meena Sodhi, *Shaw's Candida: A Critical Introduction* [New Dehli: Atlantic Publishers & Dist, 1995], p. 2). Matthew Yde's analysis of Shaw's Utopian ideals has certainly put music to that dance.

Mária Kurdi, ed., *Focus: Papers in English Literary and Cultural Studies.* Issue on Interfaces between Irish and European Theatre (2012), 144 pp. ISSN 1585-5228

Reviewed by Miklós Nyisztor

The 2012 volume of the biennial journal, *Focus: Papers in English Literary and Cultural Studies*, offers a selection of papers presented at the sixth annual conference of the Irish Society for Theatre Research (ISTR). Hosted by the Department of English Literatures and Cultures of the Institute of English Studies and the Irish Studies Research Centre at the University of Pécs, the event took place on 29-30 April 2011. The collection provides insight into the multifaceted work done by ISTR members that reaches beyond national boundaries. Two powerful studies initiate the volume, written by Marvin Carlson and Paul Murphy respectively. These two 'major essays', as Mária Kurdi rightly calls them in the 'Preface' (5), serve as portals through which one can enter the unique discursive space that enfolds in its full complexity through the rest of the papers. The notions of 'space' and 'hauntedness' as addressed in the corresponding studies form the backbone of the volume as they seem to be a prominent theme or mode of address for both the Irish and European theatre and their students. Theorizing the spatial aspect of theatre concurrent with the notion of hauntedness – regardless of how discrepant its manifestations may seem – proves especially engaging. Thus what we are offered is not only a collection of interrogative papers, but a thriving intellectual space, disclosing nuanced detail regarding the present-day dilemmas of Irish society that enter into meaningful dialogues with wider European concerns. As the papers of the volume testify, both ghosts (that often articulate repressed parts of the social or personal consciousness), and the complex and fragmented spaces (that allow for presenting conflicting truths) are recurrent theatrical forms not only in Ireland but on the continent as well.

Marvin Carlson's paper sketches the history of what he calls the 'spatial reorientation' of modern theatre studies (13). His essay captures how theatre studies gradually gave up its somewhat limited focus on the literary aspect for the benefit of a widened horizon that now includes the investigation of a variety of spaces when considering the articulation of a theatre piece. While compiling and assessing the analytic vocabulary with which theorists have approached the spatial aspect, Carlson notes a certain reluctance on the side of the students of theatre to investigate in depth the issue of space thus far. It seems even more striking, if we consider, as Carlson stresses, that the complex evocation and arrangement of different spaces (either physical or imaginary) have always been essential to theatrical practice. Theatre's intrinsic involvement with space is made clearly apparent in many contemporary productions that problematize our relation to the spatial by making use of film footage or even live video streams from either on- or off-stage. As Carlson argues, displaying the virtual, the absent and the illusory in this way, only highlights '[what] has always been a part of the theatre experience' (22).

The notion of hauntedness is introduced to the volume by Paul Murphy's paper through an investigation of how the issues of class disparity and social injustice have made their way onto the Irish stage and, if at all, into the political scene. Murphy notes a striking lack of concern for settling inequalities inherent in successive generations from the establishment of the Irish Republic onwards. Although there have been several theatrical attempts to make the grievances suffered by the lowest stratum visible (for example in the plays of J. M. Synge, Sean O'Casey, Bernard Shaw, Dermot Bolger, and Marina Carr among others), these problems seem to be evaded in the mainstream performance tradition, Murphy argues. By circumventing a direct and critical treatment with the troubling social inequalities, many times these problems were banned from the social consciousness. Nonetheless, as with all repressed material, these issues are to return and haunt present day Ireland too, as they apparently do.

Carlson's paper sets the theoretical framework for a number of essays in the volume. Miriam Haughton provides a careful analysis of the 2003 English National Theatre's world premiere of Martin McDonagh's play *The Pillowman*. Examining the various spaces presented and evoked by the production (with special attention to the set design by Scott Pask), Haughton considers the issue of power and resistance by referring to Michel Foucault. According to the French theorist, the organization of social space plays a cardinal role in exercising power over the individual, in the face of which, as Haughton argues, storytelling might mean a kind of escape. By availing himself of the 'diegetic space', the main character Katurian can challenge the dominant forces of authority and the present arrangement of society, in which he is termed and isolated as a criminal, thus finally he can make himself capable of '[providing] comfort and healing' (86) for himself. This shifting from the mimetic to the diegetic, and thus escaping from the power relations of the present and regaining agency in a fictional order, might serve as a resolution of grievances suffered by the characters and induced by the operation of power.

Eamonn Jordan's essay undertakes the task of looking at the spatial aspect of McDonagh's art, with regard to the play and productions of *A Skull in Connemara* (1997). In Jordan's essay Foucault is also invoked, this time by employing his notions of 'heterotopic spaces', 'crisis heterotopia', and 'heterotopias of deviation'. The latter imply places where healing and transcendence are completely defied, where libidinal energies get stuck and accumulate in a form of destructive indifference. They appear as a central motif and dramaturgical means in McDonagh's plays such as *A Skull in Connemara, The Beauty Queen of Leenane* (1996), or *The Lieutenant of Inishmore* (2001). Jordan assigns a liberating force to transgressing traditions that hinder the individual, thus leading to more reinvigorating approaches. With its flagrancy, the 'transgressive disinterment and quasi-sacrilegious destruction of bones' in *A Skull* (74), especially as it was staged in the Druid production, can be read as a strong objection to the 'debilitating Irish funerary practices' (75).

While one could argue that there is something inherently Irish in the inclination for dealing with ghosts in theatre (the other key issue throughout the volume), the papers scrutinizing the underlying psychological or structural patterns attest for a truly international interest. The essays of Brenda Donohue and Péter P. Müller examine the notion of hauntedness as it appears in not only Irish but various other European (Italian, Russian and Hungarian) plays. Taken as a problem of letting someone or something in, the state of being haunted is addressed in diverse ways throughout the volume. Liminal figures in the plays of the Irish playwright Marina Carr and Italian dramatist Emma Dante, much similar to haunting ghosts as Donohue argues, articulate the experience of difficulties with accepting or incorporating different aspects of their lives. Figures like the Scarecrow in Carr's *Woman and Scarecrow* (2006) or Chicho in Dante's *Vita mia* (2004) give shape to personal difficulties by embodying repressed truths – the resolution of which will eventually lead to the disappearance of these liminal characters, and thus result in a reconfiguration of the original identity now more inclusive.

The difficulty of acceptance is discussed by Péter P. Müller on an interpersonal level. He provides a 'loose kind of typology' (107) of the dramatic situations where the conflict arises from the difficulty of handling the burdensome roles of either the host or the guest. Using the Derridean term of 'hostipitality', P. Müller considers 'the essential ambivalence of the guest/host situation' (105) as it takes form in the plays and productions of J. M. Synge, Declan Hughes, and Conor McPherson in the Irish context, and of István Örkény, György Spiró, and Albert Camus in the continental one. Quoting J. Hillis Miller, Müller also adds that 'guest' and 'host' share a common linguistic root with the notion of 'ghost', which, together with *hostipitality,* add up to 'the heterogeneous experience' of the guest-host situation (106). All the discussed configurations of having guests involve a certain degree of ambivalence (or even some form of transgression) threatening the integrity of the persons in these roles, which – as Müller demonstrates – provides their dramatic potency.

Csilla Bertha's essay takes the issue of dealing with guests, hosts, or ghosts further by looking at the ethical implications. She compares Jim Nolan's *Blackwater Angel* (2001) and Brian Friel's *Faith Healer* (1979), two plays which investigate the nature of healing, faith, and theatre in an Irish context, in highly complex and self-reflective ways. The theme of the artist as a healer is a classic and universal one. However, its recurrence seems to be highly symptomatic of the contemporary ailments of society. Nolan's persistent focus on local communities with all their strengths and weaknesses, and on the artist's task to deal with this, stands in sharp contrast to the cultural aspirations of the Celtic Tiger Era, thus suggesting a warning that was perhaps not heeded in time. One is compelled to add, however, that besides its timeliness for Ireland, virtually any European country can regard ethical reconsideration of either artistic or social practice as bitingly timely.

The volume sets out to investigate possible interfaces between Irish and other European theatres. Concluding on the project, it seems apparent that nowadays theatre in Ireland and overseas increasingly utilizes its immanent capacity of creating complex spaces that can harbour previously repressed, consequently recurring, or haunting materials from deep within the individual and social unconscious. Presenting these materials in a reflective, controlled way, theatre seems to turn into a site for important healing processes. Such a (re)transformation appears requisite, and it can be read as perhaps the most prominent interface between Irish and European theatrical concerns. Complementing the sometimes-dark reality captured by the interpreters, the renewed interest of theatre-makers and students in providing space for recuperation gives reason for hope and validates the enterprise of the entire volume.

Fintan Walsh, ed., *'That was us'. Contemporary Irish Theatre and Performance* (London: Oberon Books, 2013), pp. 247, no price given.
ISBN 978-1-78319-035-5

Reviewed by Lisa Fitzgerald

The collection's title 'That was us' is taken from ANU Productions' *The Boys of Foley Street* (2012). The phrase – from a follow up to a now infamous 1975 documentary detailing the lives of four young male inner-city Dubliners – is the crux around which these various essays and recollections hinge. Commissioned by the Dublin Theatre Festival and focusing mainly on work produced between 2007 and 2013, a period in Irish history when the foundations of communities were tested by the fallout from the banking crash alongside a wave of multi-institutional collapse, the volume is in editor Fintan Walsh's words 'an attempt to understand' (16). The essays point to a need for reflection, to re-access our role in that history in order to truly claim the phrase 'that was us'.

The first section of five, 'Theatres of Testimony' centres on the idea of bearing witness to real rather than fictional events. Featuring essays from Brian Singleton, Charlotte McIvor, and Louise Lowe, the emphasis is on the performance of uncomfortable realities within Irish society. Singleton recounts his experience of attending ANU Productions' site-specific 'Monto' productions. Immersed in the performance – engaged rather than passive – the audience formed in Singleton's words 'communities of viewers' (21). The idea of audience as community is reiterated in McIvor's account of social fragmentation in Brokentalkers' *Silver Stars* (2008), *The Blue Boy* (2011), and *Have I No Mouth* (2012). McIvor argues that the plays 'wage a systematic campaign against silence in Irish society' (38). This silence permeated Irish communities when it came to issues of sexuality, particularly the repression of homosexuality, the clerical abuse of children, and alcohol abuse. The impact of this silence – institutional and endemic as it was – is highlighted in the reflections of ANU productions' artistic director Louise Lowe. Engaging directly with the audience, Lowe echoes Singleton's notion of community engagement noting that 'communion' between viewer and performer is one to 'consider deeply' (57). The moral implications of belonging to this community and taking part in how it conducts itself are evident in the testimonial nature of these productions.

'Auto/Biographical Performance' looks at how the personal, the 'self', is depicted on stage. Oonagh Murphy bemoans the lack of queer female representations in contemporary Irish theatre. She champions three plays: Tara McKevitt's *The Big Deal* (2011), Veronica Dyas' *In my Bed* (2011) and Amy Conway's *I♥Alice♥I* (2010) as worthy depictions of female sexuality within the queer narrative. Helen Meany examines biographical performances of celebrated artists. She discusses three plays, all of which premiered at the Dublin Theatre Festival: Stomach Box's site-specific *No Worst, There is None* (2009), Marina Carr's *16 Possible Glimpses* (2011) and, most recently, *The Talk of the Town* (2012) written by Emma Donoghue and directed by Annabelle Comyn. What emerges for Meany is how 'writers now fill the space previously occupied by spiritual leaders or saints' (90). The section concludes with the profound impact of Italian company, Socìetas Raffaello Sanzio, on theatre maker Dylan Tighe, an experience he likens to 'looking at a Caravaggio painting while on acid' (93). The resulting performance being experienced viscerally rather than passively consumed as the sacred space of the theatre provides a refuge for interrogating past histories.

Bodies 'not normally featured on stage' are the remit of 'Bodies out of Bounds' (7) and belong to dance and children's theatre. Making the claim that 'theatre is accessible and inclusive, but dance is inaccessible and exclusive', Michael Seaver looks at the work of Michael Keegan-Dolan, artistic director of Fabulous Beast Dance Theatre (99). John Scott, director of Irish Modern Dance Theatre, details the influence of renowned outsiders like The Living Theatre, and in particular their arrival at the Olympia for the 1978 Dublin Theatre Festival. Eimear Beardmore outlines the impact of the festival on children's theatre highlighting the work – and the physical prowess – of Theatre Lovett, noting that much of the audience is made up of 'actors coming to admire the craftsmanship' (128).

'Placing Performance' looks at contemporary Irish theatre's concern with place and space. James Hickson explores how working-class Dubliners have been represented at the theatre festival and how those depictions have evolved. This development results in an audience whose experiences 'shift to a more progressive and productive perceptivity' (154). Trish McTighe examines the upsurge in Beckett productions within Irish cultural industries, highlighting not only the ongoing critical engagement between the two but also the innovative use of space and media in recent productions. Reflecting on his experience with the festival is playwright Michael West whose work with the Corn Exchange has centred on the transformative sense that play delivers in performance.

The final section looks at touring productions. Tanya Dean and Sara Keating examine the work of Druid Theatre Company. Dean looks at the marathon play cycles that Druid have offered up – most recently Druid/Murphy (2012) – and the performance of these works not just at the theatre festival but touring smaller venues throughout the country. Keating explores how Druid, in the face of global touring and recognition, has retained their rural, west of Ireland image and ethos. Peter Crawley reflects on productions for which the Dublin Theatre Festival was 'a point of departure' and their reception abroad (226). Rough Magic's ill-fated sojourn to Torún, Poland and their subsequent success at the Edinburgh Fringe is testament to the capricious nature of audience reception. Focusing on the interaction and influence of continental Europe on Irish contemporary theatre, Crawley examines the visuality – as opposed to a traditional Irish dependence on text – of theatre makers such as Pan Pan, Brokentalkers, THEATREclub, and Fabulous Beast. These are companies creating works that challenge hegemonic Irish theatre narratives and seek out audiences interested in supporting experimental performance. Incorporating alternative tools of performance, what has emerged are the thematic similarities, different countries' same stories. While touring Brokentalker's *The*

Blue Boy – a story of institutional abuse – co-founder Feidhlim Cannon made the point that 'a lot of them don't see it as an Irish story' (222). An international partnership, *The Blue Boy* was produced by the Dublin Theatre Festival in collaboration with the LÓKAL Theatre Festival Reykjavík, the Noorderzon Performing Arts Festival Groningen, and the Korjaamo Theatre Festival Helsinki. Some histories and narratives thought of as Irish do seamlessly cross boundaries and can be deemed trans-national. The final reflection goes to Gary Keegan of Brokentalkers. Making the interesting point that one of the reasons for their international success is that they are a recognizably Irish company, Keegan acknowledges the platform that the theatre festival has offered. The event has allowed for Irish companies, not just to perform to international audiences but to immerse themselves in alternative modes of performance that has enriched the home grown theatre landscape.

The clustering of various theatre productions around a singular or annual event be it a festival or a capital of culture invites thematic strands – such as the 2012 'Your City, Your Stories' – that can dissolve when that gathering disperses. This welcome collection goes some way in redressing that. What emerges is the extraordinary part that the Dublin Theatre Festival has played in the evolution of contemporary Irish theatre. From counteracting the glaring dearth of queer female theatre performance to interrogating the representation of working class Dublin, these essays are confirmation of the importance that theatre makers attach to the annual gathering that is the Dublin Theatre Festival.

Eamonn Jordan, *From Leenane to L.A.: The Theatre and Cinema of Martin McDonagh* (Sallins, C. Kildare: Irish Academic Press, 2014), 277 pp. €27.95 (paperback) ISBN 9780716532170

Reviewed by Lilien Halada

From Leenane to L.A.: The Theatre and Cinema of Martin McDonagh investigates the richness and depth of McDonagh's world. The author discusses the playwright's work regarding topics like identity, place, violence, historical facts, psychological intentions, and clichés. In addition to exploring it critically and expanding the discussion of Martin McDonagh's oeuvre and the world of his characters, Jordan's unique contribution to scholarship in this book provides a multitude of insights into the staging of the plays, including specific interpretations by directors or actors. He writes in his introduction that it is by not only being a theatre scholar, but a spectator as well, that he gains the possibility to go into such detail (25). The examples Jordan offers throughout are relevant to such interpretations. He demonstrates the changes that occur naturally throughout the process of a single production, and describes how these changes affect a performance in such a way that one evening will be entirely different from the next. Jordan brings to our attention how small differences in the voice, a look, or a gesture in a performance can significantly change the critics' and audiences' interpretations. There are a multitude of hints, such as a play on innocence versus guilt (80) in the staging, including the specific nuances interpreted and applied by individual directors or actors. Jordan includes only a few, but very relevant examples of such interpretations. He allows the reader to see the changes occurring throughout the process of one single production. For example, when Aaron Monaghan decided to change sides of his disability as Billy, in the Druid's production of *The Cripple of Inishmann,* it did not affect his character as much as it affected the characters around him, because the actors were unsure of how to react to these changes. While it might not be obvious to the average audience member, having seen this same cast perform the play a few times, it was clear to me how the permutations resulting from such small modifications added a new level to the play.

The book is divided into three parts, each dealing with a specific aspect of McDonagh's work. 'Fictional Places, Genre, Performance and Randomness' brings to mind various arguments and criticisms that appeared as soon as the first articles on McDonagh's work had been printed, comprising the debates about McDonagh's own origins as an Englishman born to Irish parents, the inspiration for his work, and his intentions in writing these wonderfully funny and brutally wounding plays. Jordan links these questions directly to McDonagh's work itself, and also explicitly to its realization on and for the stage. The interpretation goes beyond the text. By describing those subtle movements, looks, or physical hints that appear in the performance of McDonagh's work, and explaining how they impact the meaning of the work on stage, Jordan undeniably adds to the experience of simply reading the texts.

Due to these vital details, the range of possible interpretations is expanded. This is all in addition to providing a closer look at the performances themselves, which is a rare and welcome treasure given the nature of theatre.

The second part, 'Slapstick Cultures, Dismembering Farce and Grand-Guignol Incorrectness' also deals with an array of topics that add to the continued discussion of McDonagh's work. Jordan's reference to actual performances, and not solely to the text, helps to put some of the criticism that arose at the beginning of McDonagh's career into the right perspective. He demonstrates how it is in the act of staging itself, with all the unique gestures and subtlety of interaction of characters, that these stories are truly revealed in all their potentiality. 'In Hynes's production every miniscule transaction, every micro gesture the characters perform emphasise the fact that they believe fundamentally, whether accurately or not, that there is so much at stake in every instance' (114). Although referring to *The Lonesome West*, this statement is also true of any other play directed by Hynes. Emphasizing the violence written and performed in the plays, Jordan successfully brings McDonagh's considerable cinematic output into play, setting them next to the stage-plays without making any particular deviation due to the medium in which the stories are delivered. He also points out that unlike the structure of Grand-Guignol, which is debarring empathy by some definitions as discussed in the chapter, the intermingling of 'Farce and Grand-Guignol complicate the divisions between victim and perpetrator' (155). Nevertheless, empathy with the characters is part of how McDonagh's plays work.

The third section, 'A Moral Conundrum: Psychopathology, Empathy by Way of Fragmentary Stories,' again mixes the medium of film and theatre together. Not only does Jordan discuss all three films and *The Pillowman*, but he also talks about the empathy created through the characters on many levels. However distant and irrational, pathological, and crazy a character appears to be, McDonagh uses a specific type of trick to make the character likeable. In reference to the movie *In Bruges,* Jordan points this out especially: '[T]o blend the comedy and the tragedy, the ironic awareness and the empathy, the acting needed to be particularly impressive. Interestingly, there are widely differing critical responses in relation to the performances' (193). This is something important not only for the films, but also for all of the plays. Throughout the book Jordan describes scenes out of plays or movies, stressing the performance over a plain interpretation of the characters' action via the text. This is an extremely interesting and rewarding line of inquiry, and perhaps he could have taken it even further, so as to highlight differences between individual stagings, and by doing so examining the varieties of interpretation.

In the 'Conclusion' part of the book, Jordan summarizes some of the more important criticisms levelled at McDonagh's work; specifically the aspects of it that could be called 'un-political correctness'. In this, again, Jordan refers more to the characters and less to the interpretation of them. By looking closer at the characters instead of focusing as much on scholarly interpretation, he is highlighting the clear strength of both plays and movies. They were, after all, designed to be performed and watched, and not only read and studied. Finally,

Jordan points to the tendency of unanswered questions remaining at the end of McDonagh's pieces; a 'refusal to offer confirmation' (252) that forces the audience to start thinking. Jordan argues that by making the audience aware of their own reaction to statements throughout the plays, this 'work is less about making clear-cut distinctions between protagonist and antagonism, between good and bad, punishment and revenge, but more about the collapse of determinism, carnivalesque reversals and highlighted absurdities, as McDonagh offers exceptionally accomplished insights into creativity, non-conformity, endurance, freedom, compassion, self-sacrifice, altruism and empathy'. Importantly, he adds that McDonagh's 'body of work has a great deal to say about the fundamental issues of justice and inequality for people of different beliefs, sexualities, races, genders, classes, backgrounds and abilities' (257).

This book gives a substantial assessment of many different subjects linked to the work of Martin McDonagh. Jordan continues the discussion across the playwright's oeuvre and offers a lot of interesting observations. Effectively, he encourages us to distinguish between the author and his work, and ultimately highlights the importance of individual interpretation of deliberately ambiguous stories.

